advantage interactive cd-rom

Place
Postage
Here

Irwin/McGraw-Hill
Attn: Jim Rogers, Marketing Manager
1333 Burr Ridge Parkway
Burr Ridge, IL 60521

Microsoft® Word 97 for Windows®

Sarah E. Hutchinson

Glen J. Coulthard

THE IRWIN/McGRAW-HILL ADVANTAGE SERIES FOR COMPUTER EDUCATION

Irwin
McGraw-Hill

Boston, Massachusetts Burr Ridge, Illinois Dubuque, Iowa
Madison, Wisconsin New York, New York San Francisco, California St. Louis, Missouri

Irwin/McGraw-Hill

A Division of The McGraw·Hill Companies

MICROSOFT® WORD 97 for WINDOWS®

This book is printed on acid-free paper.

2 3 4 5 6 7 8 9 0 WC/WC 9 0 9 8 7

ISBN 0-256-25996-8

Publisher: *Tom Casson*
Sponsoring editor: *Garrett Glanz*
Developmental editor: *Kristin Hepburn*
GTS production coordinator: *Cathy Stotts*
Marketing manager: *James Rogers*
Senior project supervisor: *Denise Santor-Mitzit*
Production supervisor: *Pat Frederickson*
Art director: *Keith McPherson*
Prepress buyer: *Heather D. Burbridge*
Compositor: *GTS Graphics, Inc.*
Typeface: *11/13 Bodoni Book*
Printer: *Webcrafters, Inc.*

http://www.mhcollege.com

WELCOME TO THE IRWIN ADVANTAGE SERIES

The Irwin Advantage Series has evolved over the years to become one of the most respected resources for software training in the world—to date, over 200,000 students have used one or more of our learning guides. Our instructional methodologies are proven to optimize the student's ability to learn, yet we continually seek ways to improve on our products and approach. To this end, all of our learning guides are classroom tested and critically reviewed by dozens of learners, teachers, and software training experts. We're glad you have chosen the Irwin Advantage Series!

KEY FEATURES

The following features are incorporated into the new Microsoft Office 97 student learning guides to ensure that your learning experience is as productive and enjoyable as possible:

CASE STUDIES

Each session begins with a real-world **case study** that introduces you to a fictitious person or company and describes their immediate problem or opportunity. Throughout the session, you obtain the knowledge and skills necessary to meet these challenges. At the end of the session, you are given an opportunity to solve **case problems** directly related to the case scenario.

CONCEPTS, SKILLS AND PROCEDURES

Each learning guide organizes and presents its content in logically structured session topics. Commands and procedures are introduced using **hands-on examples in a step-by-step format,** and students are encouraged to perform the steps along with the guide. These examples are clearly identified by the text design.

PERFORM THE FOLLOWING STEPS

Using this new design feature, the step progression for all hands-on examples and exercises are clearly identified. Students will find it surprisingly easy to follow the logical sequence of keystrokes and mouse clicks. No longer do you have to worry about missing a step!

END OF SESSION EXERCISES

Each session concludes with **short answer questions** and **hands-on exercises.** These comprehensive and meaningful exercises are integrated with the session's objectives; they were not added as an afterthought. They serve to provide students with opportunities to practice the session material. For maximum benefit, students should complete all the exercises at the end of each session.

IN ADDITION BOXES

These content boxes are placed strategically throughout the guide and provide information on related topics that are beyond the scope of the current discussion. For example, there are three typical categories that are visually identified by the following icons:

Integration

The key to productive and efficient use of Office 97 is in the integration features for sharing data among the applications. With a few mouse clicks, for example, you can create a PowerPoint presentation from a Word document, copy an Access database into an Excel workbook, and incorporate professional Office Art into your annual report. Under this heading, you will find methods for sharing information among the Microsoft Office 97 applications.

Advanced

In a 200+-page learning guide, there are bound to be features that are important but beyond the scope of the text. Therefore, we call attention to these features and offer suggestions on how to apply techniques or to search for more information.

Internet

The Internet is fast becoming a standard tool for gathering and exchanging information. Office 97 provides a high level of Internet connectivity, allowing the user to draw upon its vast resources and even publish documents directly on the World Wide Web. Although not every student will have a persistent Internet connection, you can review the content under this heading to learn about Office's Internet features.

Real life situations
introduce the topics

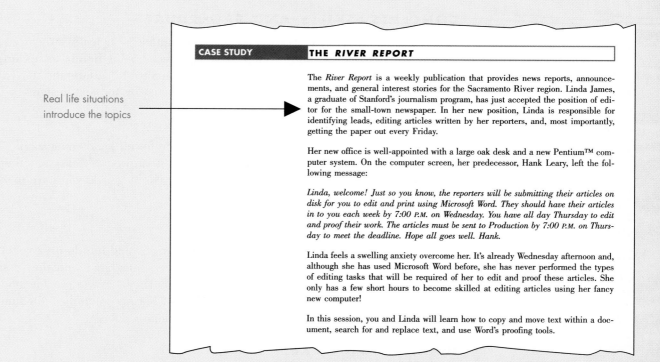

CASE STUDY   **THE *RIVER REPORT***

The *River Report* is a weekly publication that provides news reports, announcements, and general interest stories for the Sacramento River region. Linda James, a graduate of Stanford's journalism program, has just accepted the position of editor for the small-town newspaper. In her new position, Linda is responsible for identifying leads, editing articles written by her reporters, and, most importantly, getting the paper out every Friday.

Her new office is well-appointed with a large oak desk and a new Pentium™ computer system. On the computer screen, her predecessor, Hank Leary, left the following message:

Linda, welcome! Just so you know, the reporters will be submitting their articles on disk for you to edit and print using Microsoft Word. They should have their articles in to you each week by 7:00 P.M. on Wednesday. You have all day Thursday to edit and proof their work. The articles must be sent to Production by 7:00 P.M. on Thursday to meet the deadline. Hope all goes well. Hank.

Linda feels a swelling anxiety overcome her. It's already Wednesday afternoon and, although she has used Microsoft Word before, she has never performed the types of editing tasks that will be required of her to edit and proof these articles. She only has a few short hours to become skilled at editing articles using her fancy new computer!

In this session, you and Linda will learn how to copy and move text within a document, search for and replace text, and use Word's proofing tools.

Large figures guide
learning

Easy to read and
identify step-by-step
instructions

In Addition boxes
expand on topics

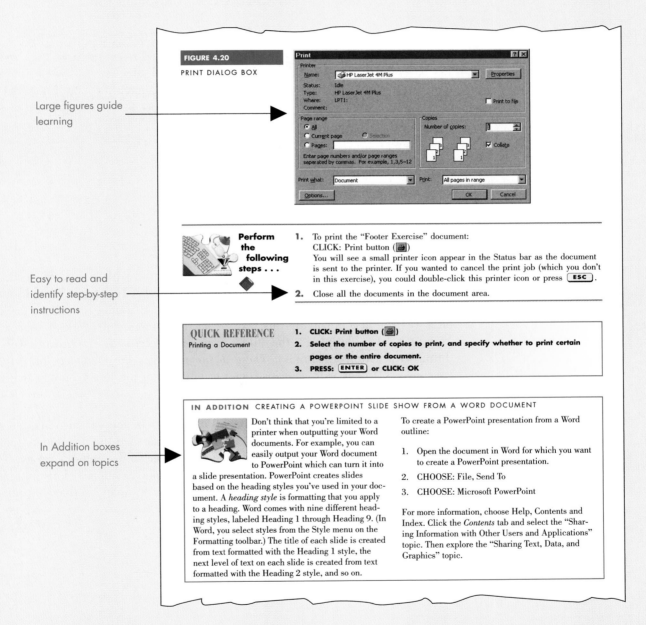

FIGURE 4.20

PRINT DIALOG BOX

Perform the following steps . . .

1. To print the "Footer Exercise" document:
   CLICK: Print button (🖨)
   You will see a small printer icon appear in the Status bar as the document is sent to the printer. If you wanted to cancel the print job (which you don't in this exercise), you could double-click this printer icon or press ESC.

2. Close all the documents in the document area.

QUICK REFERENCE

Printing a Document

1. **CLICK: Print button (🖨)**
2. **Select the number of copies to print, and specify whether to print certain pages or the entire document.**
3. **PRESS: ENTER or CLICK: OK**

IN ADDITION CREATING A POWERPOINT SLIDE SHOW FROM A WORD DOCUMENT

Don't think that you're limited to a printer when outputting your Word documents. For example, you can easily output your Word document to PowerPoint which can turn it into a slide presentation. PowerPoint creates slides based on the heading styles you've used in your document. A *heading style* is formatting that you apply to a heading. Word comes with nine different heading styles, labeled Heading 1 through Heading 9. (In Word, you select styles from the Style menu on the Formatting toolbar.) The title of each slide is created from text formatted with the Heading 1 style, the next level of text on each slide is created from text formatted with the Heading 2 style, and so on.

To create a PowerPoint presentation from a Word outline:

1. Open the document in Word for which you want to create a PowerPoint presentation.

2. CHOOSE: File, Send To

3. CHOOSE: Microsoft PowerPoint

For more information, choose Help, Contents and Index. Click the *Contents* tab and select the "Sharing Information with Other Users and Applications" topic. Then explore the "Sharing Text, Data, and Graphics" topic.

Students practice with
real life projects

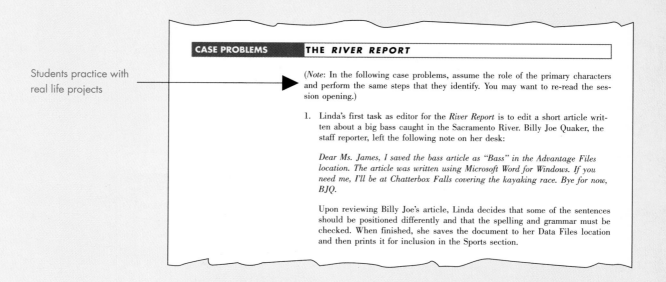

CASE PROBLEMS   **THE *RIVER REPORT***

(*Note*: In the following case problems, assume the role of the primary characters and perform the same steps that they identify. You may want to re-read the session opening.)

1. Linda's first task as editor for the *River Report* is to edit a short article written about a big bass caught in the Sacramento River. Billy Joe Quaker, the staff reporter, left the following note on her desk:

Dear Ms. James, I saved the bass article as "Bass" in the Advantage Files location. The article was written using Microsoft Word for Windows. If you need me, I'll be at Chatterbox Falls covering the kayaking race. Bye for now, BJQ.

Upon reviewing Billy Joe's article, Linda decides that some of the sentences should be positioned differently and that the spelling and grammar must be checked. When finished, she saves the document to her Data Files location and then prints it for inclusion in the Sports section.

TEXT SUPPLEMENTS

ADVANTAGE FILES

Certain hands-on examples and exercises are marked with a disk ◆ icon, indicating the need to retrieve a document file from the **Advantage Files location.** These document files may be provided to you in a number of ways: packaged on a diskette accompanying this text, or on the computer network at your school. You may also download the files from the ***Advantage Online*** Web site (http://www.irwin.com/cit/adv). *These documents files are extremely important to your success.* Check with your instructor or lab advisor for details on how to acquire the Advantage Files.

In addition to identifying the Advantage Files location, you will also need to specify a **Data Files location.** This location is used to save the documents that you create and may either be a blank diskette or a folder on the network server. Again, your instructor or lab advisor will specify the proper locations. More information on the file locations and the proper techniques for retrieving and saving information is provided inside the back cover of this book.

CD-ROM INTERACTIVE TUTORIALS

In addition to using this book, you may have access to our *Advantage Interactive* software. These interactive multimedia tutorials are fully integrated with the material from each session and make effective use of video clips, screen demonstrations, hands-on exercises, and quizzes. You will enjoy the opportunity to explore these tutorials and learn the software at your own pace. For ordering information, please refer to the coupon inside the front cover.

INSTRUCTOR'S RESOURCE KIT

For instructors and software trainers, each learning guide is accompanied by an **Instructor's Resource Kit (IRK).** This kit provides suggested answers to the short-answer questions, hands-on exercises, and case problems appearing at the end of each session. Furthermore, the IRK includes a comprehensive test bank of additional short-answer, multiple-choice, and fill-in-the-blank questions, plus hands-on exercises. You will also find a diskette copy of the Advantage Files which may be duplicated or placed on your network for student use.

SUPPORT THROUGH THE WWW

The Internet, and more specifically the World Wide Web, is an important component in our approach to software instruction for the Office 97 application series. The *Advantage Online* site at http://www.irwin.com/cit/adv is a tremendous resource for all users, providing information on the latest software and learning guide releases, download options for the Advantage Files, and supplemental files for the Instructor Resource Kits. We also introduce new methods for you to communicate with the authors, publisher, and other users of the series. As a dynamic venture, *Advantage Online* will evolve and improve over time. Please visit us to see the latest developments and contribute your valuable feedback.

NETWORK TESTING

Evaluation and assessment are important components of any instructional series. We are committed to providing quality alternatives to traditional testing instruments. With our Irwin Network Test Interactive software, instructors can select questions, create and administer tests, and then calculate grades—all on-line! Visit the *Advantage Online* site for more information on how we are progressing in this exciting area.

Before you begin

As with any software instruction guide, there are standard conventions that we use to indicate menu options, keystroke combinations, and command instructions.

MENU INSTRUCTIONS

In Office 97, all Menu bar options and pull-down menu commands have an underlined or highlighted letter in each option. When you need to execute a command from the Menu bar—the row of menu choices across the top of the screen—the tutorial's instruction line separates the Menu bar option from the command with a comma. Notice also that the word "CHOOSE" is always used for menu commands. For example, the command for quitting Windows is shown as:

CHOOSE: File, Exit

This instruction tells you to choose the File option on the Menu bar and then to choose the Exit command from the File pull-down menu. The actual steps for choosing a menu command are discussed later in this guide.

KEYSTROKES AND KEYSTROKE COMBINATIONS

When two keys must be pressed together, the tutorial's instruction line shows the keys joined with a plus (+) sign. For example, you can execute a Copy command in Windows by holding down CTRL and then pressing the letter c.

The instruction for this type of keystroke combination follows:

PRESS: CTRL +c

COMMAND INSTRUCTIONS

This guide indicates with a special typeface and color the data that you are required to type in yourself. For example:

TYPE: Income Statement

When you are required to enter unique information, such as the current date or your name, the instruction appears in italic. The following instruction directs you to type your name in place of the actual words: "your name."

TYPE: *your name*

Acknowledgments

This series of learning guides is the direct result of the teamwork and heart of many people. We sincerely thank the reviewers, instructors, and students who have shared their comments and suggestions with us over the past few years. We do read them! With this valuable feedback, our guides have evolved into the product you see before you. We also appreciate the efforts of the instructors and students at Okanagan University College who classroom tested our guides to ensure accuracy, relevancy, and completeness.

We also give many thanks to Garrett Glanz, Kristin Hepburn and Tom Casson from Irwin for their skillful management of this text. In fact, special recognition goes to all of the individuals mentioned in the credits at the beginning of this guide. And finally, to the many others who weren't directly involved in this project but who have stood by us the whole way, we appreciate your encouragement and support.

Write to us

We welcome your response to this book, for we are trying to make it as useful a learning tool as possible. Write to us in care of Garrett Glanz, Richard D. Irwin, 1333 Burr Ridge Parkway, Burr Ridge, IL 60521. Thank you.

Sarah E. Hutchinson
sclifford@mindspring.com

Glen J. Coulthard
current@junction.net

Contents

SESSION 1
Fundamentals

SESSION 2
Character and Paragraph Formatting

SESSION 3
Editing and Proofing Tools

SESSION 4
Printing and Document Management

SESSION 5
Increasing Your Productivity

APPENDIX
Microsoft Word 97 for Windows Toolbar Summary 207

INDEX   210

Microsoft Word 97 for Windows

Fundamentals

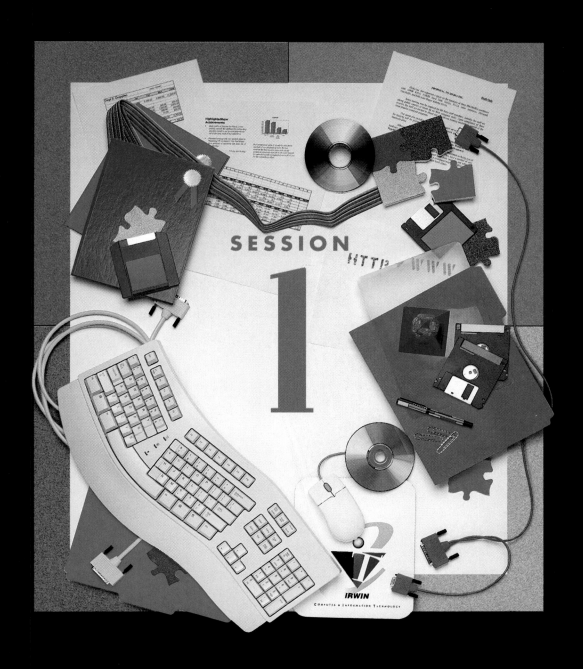

SESSION

HTTP://WWW

1

?

IRWIN

COMPUTER & INFORMATION TECHNOLOGY

SESSION OUTLINE

INTRODUCTION

Word processing is the most popular application for microcomputers. Whether you write term papers or business letters, a word processing software package lets you easily create, edit, format, and permanently store documents. Nowadays you are expected to use a computer and word processor to create your work—handwritten correspondence just isn't acceptable in formal business and educational environments. In this session, you explore the features and benefits of word processing using Microsoft Word 97 for Windows.

THE EXPERT HANDYMAN, INC.

George Perrera has lived in Irvine, California, for over 25 years. Sometimes he feels as if he knows everyone in town. His phone rarely stops ringing because he is *the* person to call when you need a household handyman. Although George has been working as a handyman for over ten years, he just recently gave his business a name: The Expert HandyMan.

George operates his business from his basement at 1990 Jillson Street. To get new clients, he relies on word-of-mouth advertising and the occasional newsletter. He currently performs an average of eight house calls per day and always seems to have more business than he can comfortably handle himself. Hoping to spend less time performing administrative tasks like creating invoices, George has purchased a new computer for his business.

Now let's focus on the problem. Invoices, invoices, invoices! With all this business, George generates eight invoices a day, nearly 40 per week. To create invoices, George uses a ball-point pen to fill out a page in a carbon-copy invoice book. He gives one copy to the customer and keeps the other for his records. George believes that it would be much more efficient to create the invoice with a word processing program, save it on the computer's hard disk, and then print a copy of the invoice for his customer. Although George has used Microsoft Windows, he doesn't know the first thing about using a word processing program.

In this session, you and George learn how to create simple documents, access Word's Help facility, edit documents, use the Undo command, and save and print your work.

INTRODUCING MICROSOFT OFFICE 97

Microsoft Office for Windows combines the most popular and exciting software programs available into a single suite of applications. In the Standard edition, Office 97 includes Microsoft Word, Microsoft Excel, Microsoft PowerPoint, and the all-new Microsoft Outlook, a desktop information tool that manages your e-mail, calendar, contacts, to-do lists, journal, and Office documents. In the Professional edition, you also get Microsoft Access, a relational database management system that fully integrates with the other Office applications. Office 97 also provides shared applications (sometimes called "servers") that let you create and insert clip art, word art, charts, and mathematical equations into your word processing documents, electronic spreadsheets, and presentations.

All software products are born with specific design goals. For Office 97, Microsoft concentrated on optimizing Office for use in Windows' 32-bit environments, including Windows 95 and Windows NT. In addition to enjoying performance improvements, Office 97 offers integration with the Internet and World Wide Web (WWW) and benefits from many usability enhancements. For example, you can name your documents using up to 250 characters, place shortcuts to documents directly on the desktop, save documents in HTML format, post documents to your corporate intranet or to the Web, use the Windows Briefcase program to compare and synchronize files, and multitask your applications with single-click functionality from the taskbar.

All of Office's primary applications use Intellisense technology, helping users to focus on their work and not on their software. Examples of Intellisense are automatic spell and grammar checking, wizards that lead you through performing basic and complex tasks, and the *Auto Web Link*, which automatically converts a World Wide Web address into a hyperlink. (*Note*: We define *hyperlinks* shortly, in the Internet Features section.) Office 97 offers additional help system features, including an animated and customizable character called the Office Assistant who provides helpful information as you work.

INTEGRATION FEATURES

Many would say that the essence of Office 97 is its ability to integrate data between applications. For example, you can include an Excel chart in a Word document, a Word document in a PowerPoint presentation, an Access database in an Excel worksheet, and so on. You can also create an object using a shared application—such as Microsoft Art Gallery, Microsoft Map, Microsoft Equation Editor, or Microsoft Organization Chart—and insert it in your document without ever leaving the current Office application.

Further blurring the line between applications, Microsoft Binder allows you to assemble, print, and distribute collections of varied documents. Like working with a real three-ring binder, you can insert documents that you create in Word, Excel, and PowerPoint into a single binder document and withdraw them. Then, you can print the contents of the binder complete with consistent headers and footers and with consecutive page numbering. A binder document also provides an easy way to transfer information from one computer to another, since all the documents are stored in a single file.

INTERNET FEATURES

One of the most exciting innovations in Office 97 is its ability to take advantage of the World Wide Web and the Internet. For those of you new to the online world, the **Internet** is a vast collection of computer networks that spans the entire planet, made up of many smaller networks connected by standard telephone lines, fiber optics, and satellites. More than just an electronic repository for information, the Internet is a *virtual community* with its own culture and tradition. The term **Intranet** refers to a private and usually secure local or wide area network that uses Internet technologies to share information. To access the Internet, you need a network or modem connection that links your computer to your account on the university's network or an independent Internet Service Provider (ISP).

Once you are connected to the Internet, you can use web browser software, such as Microsoft Internet Explorer or Netscape Navigator, to access the **World Wide Web** (WWW). The WWW provides a visual interface for the Internet and lets you search for information by simply clicking on highlighted words and images, known as **hyperlinks**. When you click a link, you are telling your computer's web browser to retrieve a page from a web site and display it on your screen. Each web page on the Internet has a unique location or address specified by its *Uniform Resource Locator* or **URL**. One example of a URL is: http://www.microsoft.com. For more information on the Internet and World Wide Web, visit your local bookstore, campus computing center, or computer users group.

Microsoft Office 97 provides a consistent set of tools for publishing documents, spreadsheets, presentations, and databases to the web and for accessing help information directly from Microsoft's corporate web site. Specifically, each Office application includes a Web toolbar that lets you quickly open, search, and browse through any document on your local computer, corporate or university Intranet, and the Internet. Furthermore, you can create your own hyperlinks and share your documents with the entire world after publishing them to a web server. As you proceed through this manual, look for the Internet integration features found in the In Addition boxes.

WORD PROCESSING WITH WORD

Word processing is the most commonly used application for microcomputers and is often cited as the primary reason for purchasing a computer. **Word processing** is the method by which documents (for example, letters, reports, and other correspondence) are created, edited, formatted, and printed using a computer. Microsoft Word is one of the most popular word processing software programs available today. Let's explore some of its features in further detail.

- *Entering text.* You create a document in Word by typing information onto the screen. As you type on the computer keyboard, text appears at the **insertion point** or cursor. When entering text, you should be aware of a feature called **word wrap**. Word wrap automatically moves the insertion point to the beginning of the next line when the end of the current line is reached.

- *Editing text.* Microsoft Word has numerous editing features to help you make corrections and modify existing documents. Two of the most important features let you insert and rearrange text. Insert mode enables you to insert text anywhere in a document. This feature works well for inserting a sentence or phrase in the middle of an existing paragraph. Also, copy and move commands allow you to change the order of paragraphs or sections in a document and limit the need to retype similar information.

- *Formatting text.* Formatting refers to changing the appearance of text in a document. There are four different levels of formatting: (a) *Character formatting* selects typefaces, font sizes, and styles for text. (b) *Paragraph formatting* specifies text alignment, line spacing, indentations, tab settings, and borders. (c) *Section formatting* lets you specify page numbers, *headers*, and *footers* for different sections or chapters of a document. (*Note*: Do not be concerned if these terms are unfamiliar; each is described in this guide.) (d) *Document formatting* specifies the overall page layout for printing.

- *Proofing tools.* Word 97 offers an integrated spell- and grammar-checking capability. When you request a Spelling and Grammar check, Word compares each word in your document to the words stored in a standard dictionary. If no match is found, the **spelling checker** typically marks the word and suggests alternative spellings or other words. Word also analyzes your document's punctuation, sentence structure, and word usage. Another writing tool in Word is the electronic thesaurus. A **thesaurus** provides a list of synonyms (and antonyms) for a given word or phrase.

- *Printing.* After creating, editing, formatting, and proofing a document, you'll want to send it to the printer. Before performing this step, make sure your computer is connected to a printer and that the printer is turned on. Your print options include printing multiple copies and limiting the print selection to specific pages. Word also allows you to preview a document on-screen before printing. Besides saving trees, this feature allows you to see the effects of formatting changes immediately without having to print the document.

- *Merging.* One of the most powerful features of Word is the ability to insert a list of names and addresses into a standard document for printing. This process, called **mail merge**, allows you to create a single document and then print personalized copies for numerous recipients. Mail merge activities are not limited, however, to producing form letters. Merging can be used to print a batch of invoices, promotional letters, or legal contracts

- *Wizards.* As you will see in this learning guide, Word employs many wizards to help you get your work done. These software features make short order of tasks that might otherwise be repetitive, time-consuming, or difficult. For example, the tasks involved in setting up a standard letter or fax cover sheet can be handled entirely by a wizard. You simply follow on-screen directions to define the document's layout.

- *"Auto" features.* Word performs a number of procedures for you automatically as you type. For example, Word's AutoCorrect feature will automatically replace "teh" with "the" and "ast he" with "as the" and ensure that your sentences begin with an uppercase letter. Other "auto" features include *AutoFormat As You Type*, *AutoComplete*, and *AutoSummarize*.

- *The Office Assistant.* Think of the Office Assistant, a component of Word's Help system, as your own personal computer guru. When you have a question about how to accomplish a task in Word, you can "talk" to the Office Assistant using typed English phrases. The Office Assistant analyzes your request and provides a resource list of potential help topics. The Assistant can also provide step-by-step instructions on how to complete a task and even perform certain tasks for you.

- *Sound.* If you have a set of speakers connected to your computer, don't be surprised if you hear sounds when you perform such common tasks as opening, closing, and saving files, deleting text, and choosing menu commands. Office 97 has added the dimension of sound to all of your Office 97 applications. You can change the sounds in the Sounds Properties dialog box of the Windows Control Panel.

Now, let's begin our journey through Microsoft Word 97.

Starting Word

This session assumes that you are working on a computer with Windows and Microsoft Word 97 loaded on the hard disk drive. Before you load Windows and Word, let's look at how to use the mouse and keyboard.

USING THE MOUSE AND KEYBOARD

Microsoft Word 97 for Windows is a complex yet easy-to-learn program. As you proceed through this guide, you will find that there are often three methods for performing the same command or procedure in Word:

- Menu   Select a command or procedure from the Menu bar.
- Mouse   Point to and click a toolbar button or use the Ruler.
- Keyboard   Press a keyboard shortcut (usually CTRL + *letter*).

Although this guide concentrates on the quickest and easiest methods, we recommend that you try the others and decide which you prefer. *Don't memorize all of the methods and information in this guide! Be selective and find your favorite methods.*

Although you may use Word with only a keyboard, much of the program's basic design and operation relies on using a mouse. Regardless of whether your mouse has two or three buttons, you use the left or primary mouse button for selecting text and menu commands and the right or secondary mouse button for displaying shortcut menus. The most common mouse actions used in Word are:

- Point   Slide the mouse on your desk to position the tip of the mouse pointer over the desired object on the screen.

- Click   Press down and release the left mouse button quickly. Clicking is used to position the insertion point in the document, select menu commands, and choose options in a dialog box.

- Right-Click   Press down and release the right mouse button. Right-clicking the mouse on text or an object displays a context-sensitive shortcut menu.

- Double-Click   Press down and release the mouse button twice in rapid succession. Double-clicking is used in Word to select text.

- Drag   Press down and hold the mouse button as you move the mouse pointer across the screen. When the mouse pointer reaches the desired location, release the mouse button. Dragging is used to select a block of text or to move objects or windows.

You may notice that the mouse pointer changes shape as you move it over different parts of the screen or during processing. Each mouse pointer shape has its own purpose and may provide you with important information. There are five primary mouse shapes you should be aware of:

▲	left arrow	Used to choose menu commands, access the toolbars, and make selections in dialog boxes.
◢	right arrow	Used to select text in the document window's Selection area.
⧗	Hourglass	Informs you that Word is occupied with another task and requests that you wait.
I	I-beam	Used to modify and edit text and to position the insertion point.
🖑	Hand	In a Help window, the hand is used to select shortcuts and definitions.

As you proceed through this guide, other mouse shapes will be explained in the appropriate sections.

Aside from being the primary input device for creating a document, the keyboard offers shortcut methods for performing commands and procedures. For example, several menu commands have shortcut key combinations listed to the right of the command in the pull-down menu. Therefore, you can perform a command by simply pressing the shortcut keys rather than accessing the Menu bar. Many of these shortcut key combinations are available throughout Windows applications.

LOADING WINDOWS

Because Windows is an operating system, it is loaded automatically into the computer's memory when you turn on the computer.

Perform the following steps . . .

1. Turn on the power switches to the computer and monitor. After a few seconds, the Windows desktop will appear (Figure 1.1). (*Note*: The desktop interface on your computer may look different from Figure 1.1.)

2. If a Welcome to Windows dialog box appears, do the following:
   CLICK: Close button (☒) in the top right-hand corner of the window

FIGURE 1.1

THE WINDOWS DESKTOP

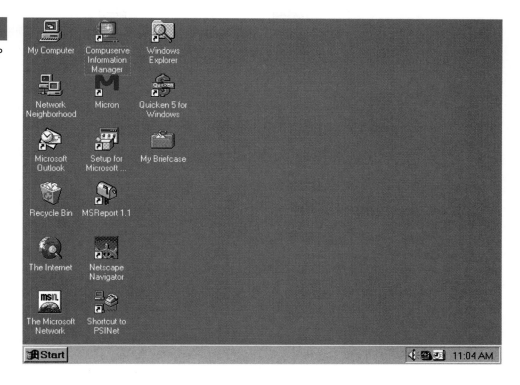

FIGURE 1.1

THE WINDOWS DESKTOP

QUICK REFERENCE
Loading Windows

Turn on your computer to load Microsoft Windows (or Microsoft Windows NT 3.51 or later).

LOADING MICROSOFT WORD 97

In this section, you load Microsoft Word.

Perform the following steps . . .

1. Point to the Start button () on the taskbar and then click the left mouse button once. The Start menu appears as a pop-up menu.

2. Point to the Programs command using the mouse. Notice that you do not need to click the left mouse button to display the list of programs in the fly-out or cascading menu.

3. Move the mouse pointer horizontally to the right until it highlights an option in the Programs menu. You can now move the mouse pointer up and down the Programs menu. Notice that you still haven't clicked the left mouse button.

4. Point to the Microsoft Word menu item and then click the left mouse button once to execute the command. After a few seconds, the Microsoft Word screen appears.

5. If the Office Assistant (shown at the right) appears:
   CLICK: Close button (☒) in its top right-hand corner

THE GUIDED TOUR

Software programs designed for Microsoft Windows, such as Word, have many similarities in screen design and layout. Each program operates in its own application window, while the letters, spreadsheets, and brochures you create appear in separate document windows. This section explores the various parts of Word, including the tools for manipulating application and document windows.

APPLICATION WINDOW

The Word screen consists of the **application window** and the **document window**. The application window (Figure 1.2) contains the Title bar, Menu bar, Standard toolbar, Formatting toolbar, Status bar, and document area. Document windows contain the actual documents that you create and store on the disk.

FIGURE 1.2

MICROSOFT WORD'S
APPLICATION WINDOW

Control icon

Title bar

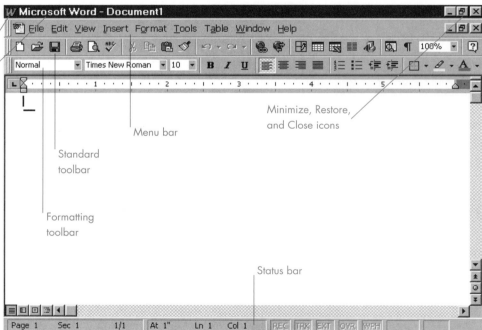

The primary components of the application window are:

Control icon (□)   Used to size and position the application window using
                        the keyboard. (*Note*: It is easier to use the mouse to
                        choose the same options available in the Control menu.)

Minimize (▬) and Maximize (▢), Restore (🗗), and Close (✖) icons	Located in the top right-hand corner of the application window, these icons are used to control the display of the application window using the mouse. (*Note*: The Maximize button doesn't appear in Figure 1.2.)
Title bar	The Title bar contains the name of the program or document file. Using a mouse, you can move a window by dragging its Title bar. (*Note*: The Office Shortcut bar may also appear in the Title bar area.)
Menu bar	Contains the Word menu commands.
Standard toolbar	The Standard toolbar displays buttons for opening and saving documents, editing text, and accessing special features using the mouse.
Formatting toolbar	The Formatting toolbar displays buttons for accessing character and paragraph formatting commands using the mouse.
Status bar	Located at the bottom of the application window and above the taskbar, the Status bar displays status or mode information and tracks your current position in a document.

Although the application window is typically maximized, you can size, move, and manipulate the Word application window on the Windows desktop to customize your work environment.

DOCUMENT WINDOW

The document window provides the viewing and editing area for a document. When Word is first loaded, this window is maximized to fill the entire document area. Figure 1.3 shows an example of a document window that is not maximized, as it would appear in the document area of Word's application window.

FIGURE 1.3

THE DOCUMENT WINDOW

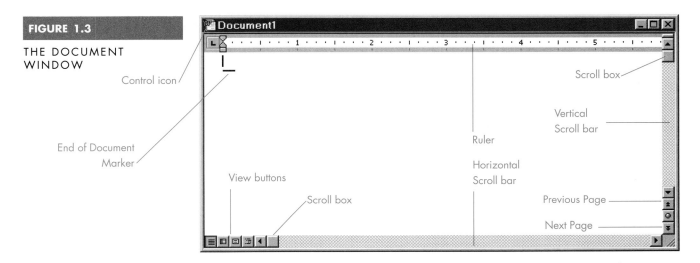

Control icon

End of Document Marker

View buttons

Scroll box

Scroll box

Ruler

Horizontal Scroll bar

Vertical Scroll bar

Previous Page

Next Page

The parts of a document window are listed below:

Control icon (▣)	Used to size and position the application window using the keyboard. (*Note*: It is easier to use the mouse to choose the same options available in the Control menu.)
Ruler	Located beneath the Formatting toolbar in a maximized window, each document window has its own Ruler that provides information about tab settings, paragraph indentations, and margins.
Scroll bars	Placed at the right and bottom borders of the document window, scroll bars facilitate moving around a document using the mouse. By dragging the scroll box along the scroll bar, you can skim quickly through a document.
View buttons	Located at the bottom left-hand corner of the document window, the View buttons let you easily switch between Normal View, Online Layout View, Page Layout View, and Outline View. The Normal View is used for the majority of your work. The Online Layout View is the best view to use if you want to read a document online. The Page Layout and Outline views provide additional features for finalizing and managing documents.
End of Document Marker and Paragraph symbol	The End of Document Marker informs you that you can not move the insertion point beyond this point in the document. Although not always displayed, the Paragraph symbol (¶) shows where you have pressed the (ENTER) key to start a new line.
Office Assistant	When you load Word, the Office Assistant appears if it was displaying when you last exited the program. The Office Assistant helps you complete tasks by providing helpful tips and answering your questions.

You should recognize some familiar components in the document window that appear in all windows. For example, the Minimize and Maximize buttons appear in the top right-hand corner of the document window. To restore a maximized document to a window, you click the Restore button (▣). To maximize the document window, you click the Maximize button (▣). Before proceeding, make sure that your document window is maximized, resembling Figure 1.2.

MENU BAR

Word commands are grouped together on the Menu bar, as shown below.

▣ File Edit View Insert Format Tools Table Window Help   _ ▣ ×

Commands in this guide are written in the following form: Edit, Copy, where Edit is the Menu bar option and Copy is the command to be selected from the pull-down menu. To execute a command, click once on the Menu bar option and then click once on the pull-down menu command. Commands that are not available for selection appear dimmed. Commands that are followed by an ellipsis (. . .) require further information to be collected in a dialog box. If you choose a command that is followed by a sideways triangle (▶), an additional pull-down menu will appear.

In this section, you practice accessing the Menu bar.

Perform the following steps . . .

1. To choose the Help command, position the tip of the mouse pointer on the word Help in the Menu bar and click the left mouse button once. A pull-down menu appears below the Help option. (*Note*: If your computer is set up to output sound, you will hear an audible click when you make a menu selection.)

2. To see the pull-down menus associated with other menu options, drag the mouse slowly to the left over the additional options on the Menu bar.

3. To leave the Menu bar without making a command selection, use one of the following methods: (a) click in the Title bar, (b) click on the current Menu bar option, (c) click in the document area, or (d) press ⌐ESC⌐ twice.

4. To display the pull-down menu for the File option:
    CHOOSE: File
    This instruction tells you to click the left mouse button once with the pointer on the File option in the Menu bar. (*Note*: All menu commands that you execute in this guide begin with the word "CHOOSE.")

5. To leave the Menu bar without making a selection:
    CHOOSE: File

SHORTCUT MENUS

Word uses context-sensitive shortcut menus for quick access to menu commands. Rather than searching for commands in the Menu bar, you position the mouse pointer on text or an object, such as a table or a graphic, and click the right mouse button. A pop-up menu appears with the most commonly selected commands for the text or object.

Now you practice accessing a shortcut menu.

Perform the following steps . . .

1. To display a shortcut or pop-up menu, position the mouse pointer over any button on the Standard toolbar and click the right mouse button. The shortcut menu at the right should appear.

2. To remove the shortcut menu from the screen, move the mouse pointer into the document area and click the left mouse button. The shortcut menu disappears.

QUICK REFERENCE
Using Shortcut Menus

1. **Position the mouse pointer over an item, such as a toolbar button.**
2. **CLICK: the right mouse button to display a shortcut or pop-up menu**
3. **CHOOSE: a command from the menu, or**
    CLICK: the left mouse button in the document area to remove it

TOOLBARS

Assuming that you haven't yet customized your Word screen, you will see the Standard and Formatting toolbars appear below the Menu bar. Word provides thirteen toolbars and hundreds of buttons[1] for quick and easy mouse access to its more popular features. Don't worry about memorizing the button names appearing in the following graphics—the majority of these buttons are explained elsewhere. You can also point at any toolbar button and pause until a yellow ToolTip appears with the button name.

The Standard toolbar provides access to file management and editing commands in addition to special features like Insert Hyperlink, Insert Table, and Columns:

The Formatting toolbar lets you access character and paragraph formatting commands:

To select additional toolbars, you point to an existing toolbar and click the right mouse button. From the shortcut menu that appears, you can display and hide toolbars by choosing their names in the pop-up menu. If a toolbar is currently being displayed, a check mark appears beside its name.

In this section, you practice displaying and hiding toolbars.

---

[1]Sometimes called *icons.*

Perform the following steps . . .

1. Position the mouse pointer over any button on the Standard toolbar.

2. CLICK: right mouse button to display the shortcut menu

3. To display the Picture toolbar:
   CHOOSE: Picture
   The new toolbar appears somewhere in the document window.

4. To remove the Picture toolbar:
   RIGHT-CLICK: Picture toolbar
   This instruction tells you to position the mouse pointer over the Picture toolbar and click the right mouse button.

5. CHOOSE: Picture
   The Picture toolbar disappears from the application window.

RULER

The Ruler (shown below) displays the tab, paragraph, and margin settings for the current line. Rather than accessing menu commands to adjust paragraph and document formatting options, you can move the symbols provided on the Ruler using the mouse.

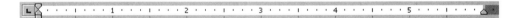

STATUS BAR

The Status bar (shown below) provides editing and status information for a document, including the current page number, section number, and total number of pages. The insertion point's current depth from the top of the page is displayed in inches, along with the line and column numbers.

The Status bar also provides some helpful information. For example, when "OVR," which stands for Overtype mode, appears dimmed in the Status bar, Word is in Insert mode. You can toggle between Overtype and Insert modes by double-clicking the "OVR" indicator on the Status bar. The book icon, which we describe later in this session, is used to correct spelling and grammar errors.

DIALOG BOX

A dialog box is a common mechanism in Windows applications for collecting information before processing a command or instruction (Figure 1.4). In a dialog box, you indicate the options you want to use and then click the OK button when you're finished. Dialog boxes are also used to display messages or to ask for the confirmation of commands.

FIGURE 1.4

A DIALOG BOX

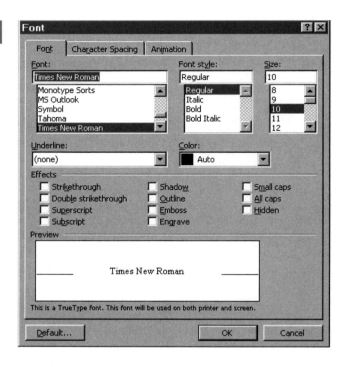

A dialog box uses several methods for collecting information. We describe each method in Table 1.1.

Most dialog boxes provide a question mark button ([?]) near the right side of the Title bar. If you have a question about an item in the dialog box, click the question mark and then click the item to display some helpful information. You should also know that dialog boxes have a memory. For example, the tab that appears when you exit the dialog box will be selected the next time you open the dialog box.

THE WINDOWS TASKBAR

The Windows taskbar is usually located on the bottom of your screen below the Status bar. (*Note*: We say "usually" because you can move the taskbar around on your desktop.) Each application that you are currently working with is represented by a button on the taskbar. To switch between applications, click the appropriate application button on the taskbar. At this point, you should see a button for Microsoft Word on the taskbar.

GETTING HELP

Word provides several **context-sensitive help** features and a comprehensive library of online documentation. Like many developers trying to minimize the retail price of software and maximize profits, Microsoft has stopped shipping volumes of print-based documentation in favor of disk-based Help systems. However, a Help system is only as good as the search tools that it provides. Fortunately for us, Windows gives developers the tools and capability to create consistent and easy-to-use

TABLE 1.1

Parts of a
Dialog Box

Name	Example	Action
Check box	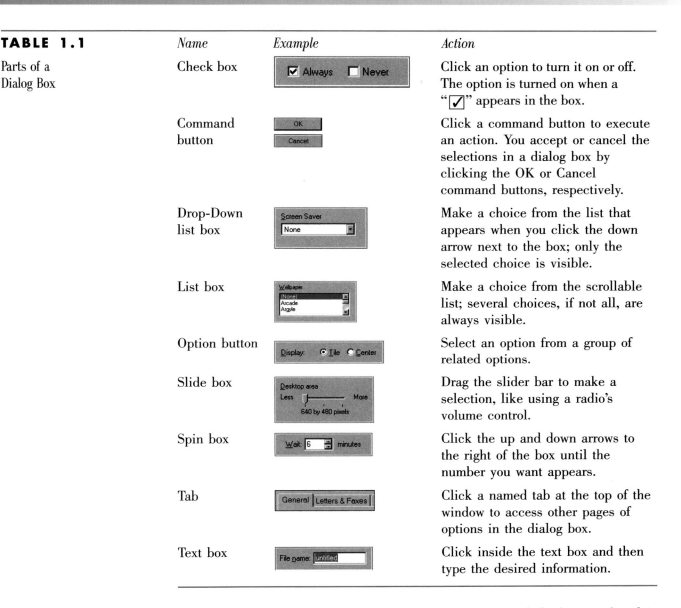	Click an option to turn it on or off. The option is turned on when a "☑" appears in the box.
Command button		Click a command button to execute an action. You accept or cancel the selections in a dialog box by clicking the OK or Cancel command buttons, respectively.
Drop-Down list box		Make a choice from the list that appears when you click the down arrow next to the box; only the selected choice is visible.
List box		Make a choice from the scrollable list; several choices, if not all, are always visible.
Option button		Select an option from a group of related options.
Slide box		Drag the slider bar to make a selection, like using a radio's volume control.
Spin box		Click the up and down arrows to the right of the box until the number you want appears.
Tab		Click a named tab at the top of the window to access other pages of options in the dialog box.
Text box		Click inside the text box and then type the desired information.

Help systems. This section describes the context-sensitive help features found in Word and then describes where to find more detailed information using the Help Topics window.

CONTEXT-SENSITIVE HELP

Context-sensitive help refers to a software program's ability to retrieve and present helpful information reflecting your current position in the program. In Word, you can access context-sensitive help for menu options, toolbar buttons, and dialog box items. The help information is presented concisely in a small pop-up window that you can remove with the click of the mouse. This type of help lets you access information quickly and then continue working without interruption. Table 1.2 describes some methods for accessing context-sensitive help while working in Word.

TABLE 1.2	*To display . . .*	*Do this . . .*
Displaying context-sensitive Help information	A description of a dialog box item	Click the question mark button (⬜?) in a dialog box's Title bar and then click an item in the dialog box. A helpful description of the item appears in a pop-up window. Additionally, you can often right-click a dialog box item to display its description.
	A description of a menu command	Choose Help, What's This? from the Menu bar and then choose the desired command using the question mark mouse pointer. Rather than executing the command, a helpful description of the command appears in a pop-up window.
	A description of a toolbar button	Point to a toolbar button to display its ToolTip label; a full description of the toolbar button also appears in the Status bar. You can also choose Help, What's This? from the Menu bar and then click a toolbar button to display more detailed help information in a pop-up window.

Now you will access context-sensitive help.

Perform the following steps . . .

1. In the next few steps, you practice choosing Help, What's This? to access Help for the File, New command and one of the toolbar buttons. Let's start with the File, New command.
CHOOSE: Help

2. To activate the question mark mouse pointer:
CHOOSE: What's This?

3. CHOOSE: File, New
Rather than executing the command, Word provides a description of the command.

4. After reading the description, close the window by clicking on it once.

5. To display information about a toolbar button:
CHOOSE: Help, What's This?
CLICK: Save button (🖫) on the Standard toolbar
The following pop-up window appears:

> **Save (File menu)**
> Saves the active file with its current file name, location, and file format.

6. CLICK: the pop-up window once to remove it

7. Word also provides a special Help tool called the Office Assistant. The Office Assistant watches your keystrokes as you work and offers suggestions and shortcuts. The Office Assistant may appear as a paperclip (by default) or as another character. To display the Office Assistant:
CLICK: Office Assistant button (⬚)
The Office Assistant and its associated tip window appear. Your screen should appear similar to Figure 1.5.

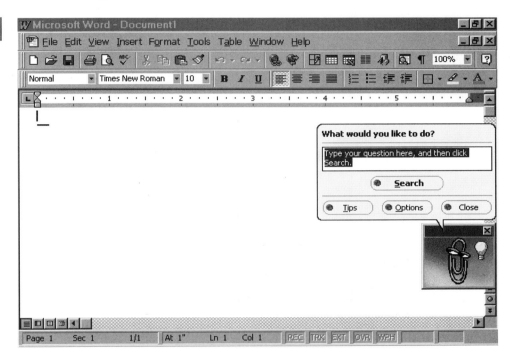

8. To type in a question about page numbers, perform the following steps:
TYPE: insert page numbers in a document

9. To display information about your topic, you click the Search button.
CLICK: Search button in the tip window
A list of related topics appears.

10. To close the tip window:
CLICK: Close button

11. The Office Assistant box, without the tip window, appears in the document window. By simply clicking the animated character, the Office Assistant will display information about the procedure you are performing. To illustrate, do the following:
CHOOSE: Format, Columns

12. To obtain additional information about creating columns:
CLICK: Office Assistant character
A list of topics related to columns appears in the tip window.

13. To remove the Office Assistant box and tip window:
CLICK: Close icon (⊠) in the Office Assistant dialog box

14. To close the Columns dialog box:
CLICK: Cancel command button

Occasionally an illuminated light bulb will appear in the Office Assistant box. This is the Office Assistant's way of telling you it has a new tip or suggestion. You tell the Office Assistant that you want to view the tip by clicking the light bulb.

QUICK REFERENCE
Displaying Context-Sensitive Help

1. **CHOOSE: Help, What's This?**
2. **Using the question mark mouse pointer, select the desired item for which you want to display a help pop-up window:**
   - **CHOOSE: a menu command, or**
   - **CLICK: a toolbar button, or**
   - **CLICK: a dialog box item**

HELP TOPICS WINDOW

The primary way that you access Word's Help system is by choosing the Help, Contents and Index command from the menu. This command displays the Help Topics window, as shown in Figure 1.6. You can think of the Help Topics window as the front door to Word's vast help resources.

FIGURE 1.6

HELP TOPICS WINDOW: CONTENTS TAB

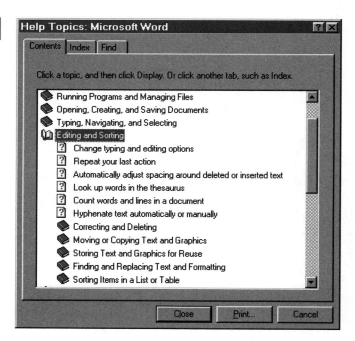

The Help Topics window provides three different tools, each on its own tab, to help you find the information you need quickly and easily. You point to and click a tab using the mouse to make the tab active in the window. Refer to the following tab descriptions to determine which tool you should use when requiring assistance:

• *Contents* tab   Displays a list of help topics organized as a hierarchy of books and pages. Think of this tab as the Table of Contents for the entire Help system. You navigate through categories by double-clicking book icons (📖) until reaching the desired help topic (?). Notice in Figure 1.6 that there are three different types of icons displayed:

📖 represents a help category; double-click a book icon to view the books and topics it contains

📖 represents an open category that is currently displaying its contents; double-click an open book icon to close (or collapse) the book

? represents a help topic; double-click a topic icon to display a help window

• *Index* tab   Displays an alphabetical list of keywords and phrases, similar to a traditional book index. To search for a topic using this tab, you type a word (or even a few letters) into the text box, which, in turn, makes the list box scroll to the first matching entry in the index. When the desired entry appears in the list box, double-click it to display the help topic. If a keyword has more than one associated topic, a Topics Found window appears and you can select a further topic to narrow your search.

• *Find* tab   Provides the ability to conduct a full-text search of the Help system for finding a particular word or phrase. Although similar to the *Index* tab, this tab differs in its ability to look past indexed keywords and search the help text itself.

When you double-click a help topic, it is displayed in a *secondary* window. You may find that secondary windows include some unfamiliar buttons, like 📎 and 📎, embedded in the help text. The 📎 symbol, which we'll call the Chiclet button, represents a "See Also" link that you can click to move to a related help topic. The 📎 symbol, called the Show Me button, initiates the command you're interested in. You may also notice that some words or phrases in the help window have a dotted underline. If you click such a word or phrase, a definition pop-up window appears.

Now you will access the Help Topics window.

Perform the following steps . . .

1. To access the Help Topics window:
   CHOOSE: Help, Contents and Index

2. CLICK: *Contents* tab
   Your screen should now appear similar to Figure 1.6, except that your book categories will appear collapsed. (*Note:* The Help Topics window remembers the tab that was selected when it was last closed. It will automatically

return to this tab the next time you access the Help system. For example, if you close the Help Topics window with the *Index* tab active, it will again appear active the next time you display the window.)

3. To display the contents of a book:
DOUBLE-CLICK: "📖 Editing and Sorting" book
(*Note*: You can double-click the book icon (📖) or the book's title. If you find it difficult to double-click using the mouse, you can also select or highlight the book by clicking it once and then click the Display command button.) This particular book contains six topic pages and five additional book categories.

4. To further clarify the search:
DOUBLE-CLICK: "📖 Correcting and Deleting" book
Notice that this book contains multiple topics.

5. To display a help topic:
DOUBLE-CLICK: "❓ Automatically correct text" topic
The Help Topics window is removed from view and a secondary window appears with the topic information.

6. To print the help topic:
RIGHT-CLICK: anywhere in the help text of the secondary window
CHOOSE: Print Topic (as shown in Figure 1.7)
(*Note*: You can also print help information directly from the *Contents* tab. If you select a book by clicking on it once and then click the Print command button, the entire book (including the additional book categories that may be contained within the book) is sent to the printer. If you select an individual topic and click Print in the Help Topics window, only the highlighted topic is sent to the printer.)

FIGURE 1.7

DISPLAYING A HELP
TOPIC AND A SHORTCUT
MENU

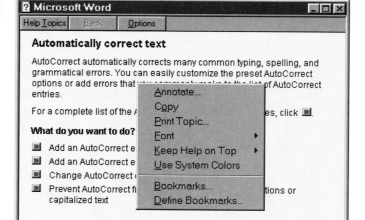

7. In the Print dialog box that appears:
- CLICK: OK command button to print the topic, or
- CLICK: Cancel command button if you do not have a printer

Whatever your selection, you are returned to the secondary window. (*Note*: If you selected to print the topic and your computer does not have a printer connected, you may be returned to Word with an error message. In this case, choose Help, Contents and Index to redisplay the Help Topics window and then proceed to Step 10.)

8. To close the secondary window and return to the Help Topics window:
CLICK: Help Topics button (immediately under the Title bar)

9. To close the current book:
CLICK: ▲ on the vertical scroll bar repeatedly
DOUBLE-CLICK: "📖 Editing and Sorting" book
Notice that the list of books and topics is collapsed under the book icon.

10. Let's search for some information using the keyword index:
CLICK: *Index* tab

11. To find the topics related to Word's AutoFormat feature:
TYPE: `autoformat`
The list automatically scrolls to highlight "AutoFormat."

12. In the topic list:
DOUBLE-CLICK: AutoFormat
A secondary window appears with additional topics.

13. In the Topics Found window:
DOUBLE-CLICK: "Turn automatic changes on or off"

14. You may have noticed that a term in this secondary window appears with a dotted underline. To view this definition term, do the following:
CLICK: "AutoText" with the hand mouse pointer (🖑)
A pop-up window appears with a definition.

15. After reading the help text, remove the definition pop-up window:
CLICK: the pop-up window once

16. To return to the Help Topics window:
CLICK: Help Topics button

17. Let's close the Microsoft Word Help system. To do so:
CLICK: Cancel command button (in the lower right-hand corner)
The Help Topics window is removed. (*Remember*: The next time you open the Help Topics window, the *Index* tab will be selected.)

QUICK REFERENCE
Searching for Help Using the Help Topics Window

1. **To display the Help Topics window:**
   CHOOSE: Help, Contents and Index

2. **CLICK: *Contents* tab to navigate a hierarchical Help system**
   CLICK: *Index* tab to search for a word or phrase in a keyword index
   CLICK: *Find* tab to conduct a full-text search of the Help system

---

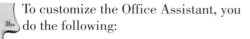

IN ADDITION CUSTOMIZING THE OFFICE ASSISTANT

To customize the Office Assistant, you do the following:

1. Ensure that the Office Assistant box appears.

2. RIGHT-CLICK: the Office Assistant character in the box

3. CHOOSE: Choose Assistant from the menu

4. Use the *Gallery* tab to select your favorite Office Assistant.

5. Select or remove features in the *Options* tab.

6. When finished, press **ENTER** or CLICK: OK

CREATING A DOCUMENT

Creating a document in Word is easy. You type information onto the screen, save the document to the disk, and, if desired, send it to the printer. Before you begin typing, make sure that you have a blinking insertion point in the upper left-hand corner of the document window. This marks the location where text is inserted. Below the insertion point, you should see a horizontal black bar called the **End of Document Marker**. As you enter information, this marker automatically moves downward.

In the next few sections, you will create the paragraph appearing in Figure 1.8.

FIGURE 1.8

PRACTICE PARAGRAPH

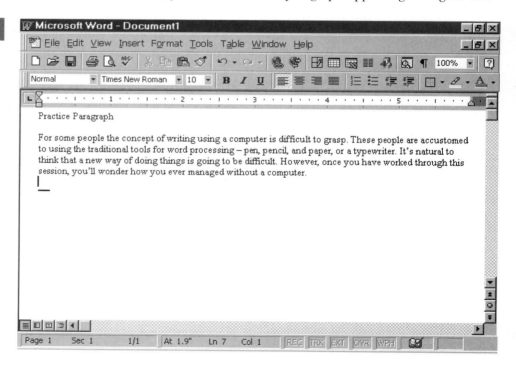

BEFORE YOU BEGIN: CHECKING YOUR "AUTO" SETTINGS

Before you create the document in Figure 1.8, let's look at the AutoCorrect, Auto-Format, and spelling and grammar settings on your computer. If necessary, we recommend that you change the settings to match those shown in Figures 1.9, 1.10, and 1.11. (*Note*: These settings correspond to Word's default settings; that is, these settings are in effect after Word is first installed.) Then, the Figures in this learning guide will match what you view on your screen.

Perform the following steps . . .

1. To check the AutoCorrect settings:
CHOOSE: Tools, AutoCorrect from the Menu bar
CLICK: *AutoCorrect* tab
Your screen should now appear similar to Figure 1.9.

FIGURE 1.9

THE AUTOCORRECT DIALOG BOX: AUTOCORRECT TAB

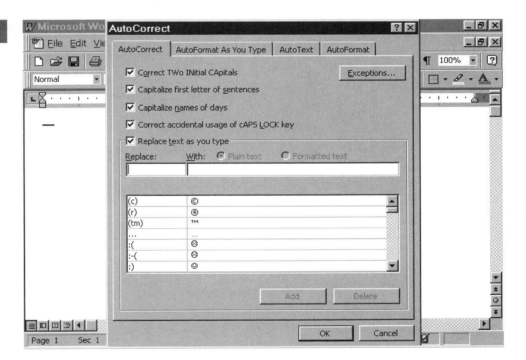

2. If necessary, change the settings in the AutoCorrect tab to match those in Figure 1.9. To select or deselect a check box, point to the box and click the left mouse button.

3. To check the "AutoFormat As You Type" settings:
CLICK: *AutoFormat As You Type* tab
Your screen should now appear similar to Figure 1.10.

FIGURE 1.10

THE AUTOCORRECT
DIALOG BOX:
AUTOFORMAT AS YOU
TYPE TAB

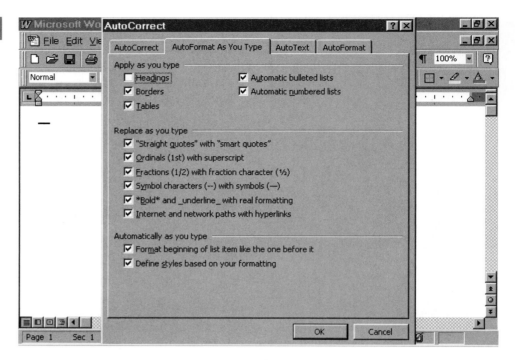

4. If necessary, change the settings in the *AutoFormat As You Type* tab to match those in Figure 1.10. (*Note*: We describe the options available in the *AutoFormat As You Type* tab later in this guide.)

5. To close the AutoCorrect dialog box:
CLICK: OK button

6. To check the spelling and grammar settings:
CHOOSE: Tools, Options
CLICK: *Spelling & Grammar* tab
Your screen should now appear similar to Figure 1.11.

FIGURE 1.11

THE OPTIONS DIALOG
BOX: SPELLING &
GRAMMAR TAB

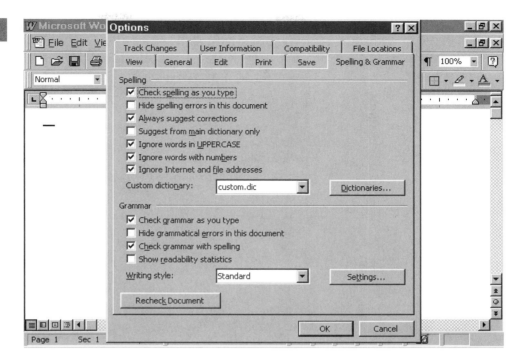

7. If necessary, change the settings in the *Spelling & Grammar* tab to match those in Figure 1.11. (*Note:* We describe the options available in the *Spelling & Grammar* tab later in this guide.)

8. To close the Options dialog box:
CLICK: OK button

INSERTING TEXT

To illustrate the fundamentals of inserting text, this section leads you through an exercise for editing the words "Practice Paragraph." You will also learn about Word's AutoCorrect feature which automatically corrects simple typographical errors in spelling and capitalization. For example, you can type "teh" and Word replaces the text with "the" as soon as you press the Space Bar. For typographical errors that aren't so straightforward, don't be surprised if Word displays a wavy red underline beneath the offending word. Because Word checks your spelling and grammar as you type, some words in your document may appear with a red (spelling error) or green (grammar error) wavy underline. For now, ignore any underlines that you may encounter.

Perform the following steps . . .

1. TYPE: `Paragraph`
The insertion point appears one character to the right of the word "Paragraph."

2. To move the insertion point back to the beginning of the line:
PRESS: (**HOME**)
The insertion point should now appear to the left of the "P" in "Paragraph."

3. Make sure that the letters OVR in the Status bar appear dimmed. This tells you that Word's current mode is Insert mode and not Overtype mode. If the letters OVR are not dim, double-click the letters in the Status bar before continuing. Type the following, exactly as it appears:
TYPE: **PRactice**
PRESS: Space Bar
Notice that Word's AutoCorrect feature automatically corrected your capitalization error at the beginning of the word. Also, the Insert mode let you insert text and spaces at the current position by simply typing the characters and pressing the Space Bar. The existing information was pushed to the right.

4. To illustrate the difference between Insert mode and Overtype mode, position the insertion point to the left of the letter "P" in the word "Practice."

5. Locate OVR, the abbreviation for Overtype mode, on the Status bar.
DOUBLE-CLICK: OVR
The letters OVR appear highlighted (not dimmed) in the Status bar.

6. TYPE: **My**
The word "My" overwrites the first two characters of "Practice."

7. To toggle back to Insert mode:
DOUBLE-CLICK: OVR in the Status bar
The letters OVR should now appear dimmed.

8. Let's complete the phrase:
PRESS: Space Bar to insert a space
TYPE: **Pr**
The line should now read "My Practice Paragraph."

9. The (**ENTER**) key inserts blank lines into a document and signifies the end of a paragraph. To illustrate, position the insertion point to the left of the letter "P" in the word "Paragraph."

10. PRESS: (**ENTER**) four times
The word "Paragraph" moves down with the insertion point and blank lines are inserted into the document.

In the next section, you learn how to delete blank lines from a document.

QUICK REFERENCE
Inserting Text

- **Insert text into a document by typing.**
- **Insert spaces between words by pressing the Space Bar in Insert mode.**
- **Insert blank lines in a document by pressing the (ENTER) key.**
- **To toggle between Insert and Overtype modes:**
  PRESS: (INSERT) or DOUBLE-CLICK: OVR in the Status bar

DELETING TEXT

The (BACKSPACE) and (DELETE) keys are the most common keystrokes for removing information from a document one character at a time. Let's now practice using these keystrokes.

Perform the following steps . . .

1. To quickly move to the top of the document:
   PRESS: (CTRL) + (HOME)
   This instruction tells you to press and hold down the (CTRL) key and tap (HOME) once. You then release both keys. The insertion point jumps to the first column of the first line in the document. (*Note:* If your keyboard does not have separate arrow keys, ensure that the Num Lock status is off before performing this keystroke combination.)

2. To move to the end of the line:
   PRESS: (END)

3. In order to get the word "Paragraph" back to its original location, you must delete the blank lines.
   PRESS: (DELETE) four times

4. To illustrate the use of the (BACKSPACE) key, position the insertion point to the left of the word "Practice" using the mouse or keyboard.

5. PRESS: (BACKSPACE) three times
   The word "My" and the space are deleted. The text now reads "Practice Paragraph" once again.

6. To move the insertion point down two lines without moving the text:
   PRESS: (END) to move to the end of the line
   PRESS: (ENTER) twice
   The insertion point is now in the correct position for you to begin typing the practice paragraph.

QUICK REFERENCE
Deleting Text

- **PRESS:** (DELETE) to delete text to the right of the insertion point
- **PRESS:** (BACKSPACE) to delete insertion point

WORD WRAP

The word wrap feature of Word allows you to continuously type without having to press the (ENTER) key at the end of each line. If you have worked on a typewriter, resist the temptation to hit a carriage return ((ENTER)) when the right margin approaches. Word will take you to the next line automatically. In this section, you complete the practice paragraph.

Perform the following steps . . .

1. TYPE: `For some people the concept of writing using a computer is difficult to grasp. These people are accustomed to using the traditional tools for word processing -- pen, pencil, and paper, or a typewriter. It's natural to think that a new way of doing things is going to be difficult. However, once you have worked through this session, you'll wonder how you ever managed without a computer.`

2. PRESS: `ENTER`
   Your screen should now appear similar to Figure 1.8. Notice that Word automatically formatted your double-dash into a continuous dash, called an *em dash*.

QUICK REFERENCE
Word Wrap

When typing a paragraph, do not press the `ENTER` key at the end of each line. The `ENTER` key is used only to end a paragraph or to insert a blank line in a document.

IN ADDITION HYPHENATING WORDS

Words sometimes wrap to the next line in such a way that your paragraphs have a very ragged right margin. You can hyphenate words yourself or direct Word to hyphenate long words where needed.

To access the hyphenation feature, choose Tools, Language, Hyphenation from the Menu bar. For more information, choose Help, Contents and Index. Click the *Index* tab, and then type **hyphenation.**

AUTOMATIC SPELL AND GRAMMAR CHECKING

If Word's "Check spelling as you type" and "Check grammar as you type" features have been selected (see the "Before You Begin" section), one or two words in your document may already be marked with a wavy underline.

Red underline indicates that the Spelling Checker can't find a match for a word in its main dictionary. It may be that the typed word isn't misspelled at all; perhaps it's a proper name like "Carlos Rodriguez." To correct a misspelled word, point to the word using the mouse and then right-click. A shortcut menu will appear with a list of suggested correct spellings and a few additional options. You can either select the correct word from the list, choose the Ignore All command if the word is spelled correctly, or edit the word yourself. Use a similar procedure to correct grammar errors.

To correct all of your spelling and grammar errors at once, use the book icon on the Status bar. If your document is free of spelling and grammar errors, a check mark will appear on the book icon. Otherwise, an "☒" will appear. To jump through the spelling and grammar errors in a document, double-click the book icon.

In this section, you practice correcting a spelling error and a grammar error.

Perform the following steps . . .

1. In this step, you will force a spelling error in the first line of the practice paragraph. Edit the word "concept" so that it becomes "concpt."

2. Click once with the mouse in another part of the paragraph. Notice that a red wavy underline appears beneath the misspelled word.

3. To correct the word, point to the word and then right-click using the mouse. Your screen should now look similar to Figure 1.12.

FIGURE 1.12

THE SPELLING SHORTCUT MENU

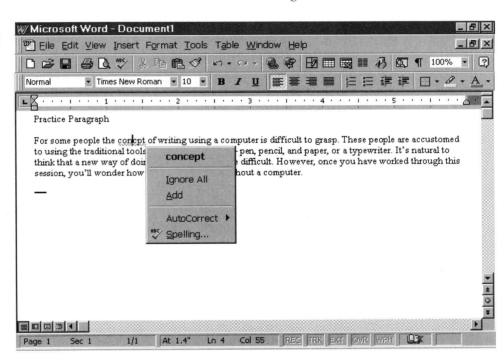

4. Using the mouse, choose the word "concept" in the menu. The word "concept" should have replaced "concpt" in the document.

5. To create a grammar error, delete the apostrophe (') in the word "It's" located at the beginning of the third sentence.

6. Click the mouse pointer in another part of the paragraph. A green wavy underline should appear.

7. To correct the error, point to the word and then right-click using the mouse.

8. Using the mouse, choose the word "It's" from the menu. The word "It's" should have replaced "It's" in the document.

9. On your own, correct any spelling and grammar errors that may still exist in your document by double-clicking the book icon on the Status bar.

USING THE UNDO COMMAND

The **Undo command** allows you to cancel the last several commands you performed in a document. There are three methods for executing the Undo command. You can choose Edit, Undo from the menu, press the keyboard shortcut of **CTRL** +z, or click the Undo button (🔄) on the Standard toolbar.

Let's practice using the Undo button (🔄):

Perform the following steps . . .

1. Make sure that you are in Insert mode (the letters OVR should appear dimmed in the Status bar) and then insert another blank line at the end of the document:
    PRESS: **CTRL** + **END** to move the cursor to the end of the document
    PRESS: **ENTER**

2. TYPE: `This is a test of the Undo command.`

3. To undo the typing you just performed:
    CLICK: Undo button (🔄) on the Standard toolbar
    (*CAUTION*: You place the tip of the mouse pointer over the curved arrow on the left side of the button, as opposed to the downward pointing arrow, before clicking the left mouse button.)

4. TYPE: `This is a test of the Menu bar method.`

5. To undo the typing again:
    CHOOSE: Edit, Undo Typing

6. To view all the actions that you can undo:
    CLICK: down arrow beside the Undo button (🔄)
    To see additional Undo actions, drag the scroll box downward.

7. To remove the drop-down list without selecting an item:
    CLICK: down arrow beside the Undo button (🔄) again

SAVING AND CLOSING A DOCUMENT

When you are creating a document, it exists only in the computer's RAM (random access memory), which is highly volatile.[2] To permanently store your work, you must save the document to the hard disk or to a floppy diskette. Saving your work to a disk is similar to placing it into a filing cabinet. For important documents (ones that you cannot risk losing), you should save your work every 15 minutes, or whenever you're interrupted, to protect against an unexpected power outage or other catastrophe.

To save a document to a disk, you click the Save button (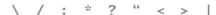) on the Standard toolbar or you select the File, Save command from the menu. If you haven't saved the document before, a dialog box appears with a suggested filename. You can either accept the suggested filename or type in a new name. When naming a file for use with Windows, you can use up to 255 characters, including spaces. You can't use the following characters in filenames:

$$\backslash \quad / \quad : \quad * \quad ? \quad " \quad < \quad > \quad |$$

When you are finished typing the filename, press **ENTER** or click the Save command button. As the document is being written to the disk, a series of boxes appears in the Status bar indicating its progress.

In the next few steps, you will save the document to one of the following locations:

- *Advantage Files location*—This location may be on a diskette, in a folder on your local hard drive, or in a folder on a network server. The Advantage Files are the document files that have been created for you and that you will retrieve in the remaining exercises in this guide.

- *Data Files location*—This location may also be on a diskette, in a hard drive folder, or in a network folder. It may even be the same disk or folder where you keep the Advantage Files. You will save the documents that you create or modify to the Data Files location.

> **IMPORTANT:** *Before continuing, ensure that you know the location of your Advantage Files and where to store your Data Files. If necessary, ask your instructor or lab assistant for additional information.*

Now let's save the current document.

Perform the following steps . . .

1. Make sure that you have identified the location for storing your data files. If you require a diskette, place it into the diskette drive now.

---

[2]RAM is wiped clean when you turn off your computer or experience a power failure.

2. CLICK: Save button (🖫)
The Save As dialog box should appear (Figure 1.13); the filenames and directories may differ from your dialog box.

FIGURE 1.13

THE SAVE AS
DIALOG BOX

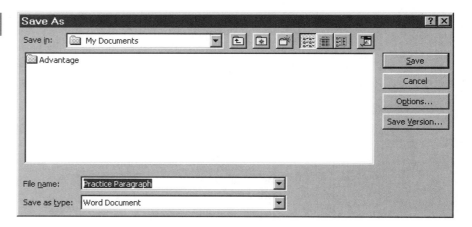

3. To specify a filename for the document, you would type it into the *File name* text box. Since the name "Practice Paragraph" already appears in the *File name* text box, let's move to the next step.

4. To specify where the document will be saved, do the following:
CLICK: down arrow beside the *Save in* drop-down list box
SELECT: *your Data Files location*
PRESS: (**ENTER**) or CLICK: Save command button
Note: In this guide, we save documents to the "My Documents" folder on the hard disk and retrieve documents from the "Word97" sub-folder, which is located at the following path:
\My Documents\Advantage\Word97

5. When you are finished working with a document, you close the file to free up valuable RAM. To close the "Practice Paragraph" file:
CHOOSE: File, Close

There are times when you'll want to save an existing document under a different filename. For example, you may want to keep different versions of the same document on your disk. Or, you may want to use one document as a template for future documents that are similar in style and format. Rather than retyping an entirely new document, you can retrieve an old document file, edit the information, and then save it under a different name using the File, Save As command. If you want to replace the old file instead, choose File, Save or click the Save button (🖫).

IN ADDITION SAVING A DOCUMENT AS A PROTECTED FILE

If you're sharing your computer with other people, but don't want anyone else to be able to look at or modify your files, consider assigning a password to your individual files. Before opening or modifying a protected file, you must type in the correct password.

To assign a password to a document, choose File, Save As and then click the Options command button. The *Save* tab should already be selected with the file sharing options appearing at the bottom.

For more information, choose Help, Contents and Index. Click the Index tab and then type in `password-protected documents.`

IN ADDITION SAVE A DOCUMENT TO AN FTP SITE

If you want your document to be accessible to others on the Internet, consider saving it to an FTP site. *FTP (File Transfer Protocol)* makes it possible for users to transfer documents over the Internet. You can save to an FTP site if your computer has an Internet connection that supports saving files. To save to an FTP site:

1. CHOOSE: File, Save As
2. SELECT: Internet Connections (FTP) from the Save in drop-down list
3. DOUBLE-CLICK: the site you want to save to (*Note:* You can add FTP sites to the list by selecting Add/Modify FTP Locations in the file area.)
4. TYPE: a name for your document
5. PRESS: **ENTER** or CLICK: Save command button

IN ADDITION SAVE AS HTML

To publish your Word document on the Web, you must save it in an HTML format first. *HTML (Hypertext Markup Language)* is a system for marking up documents so they can be viewed on the World Wide Web. To save a document as an HTML document:

CHOOSE: File, Save as HTML

(*Note:* It is a good idea to choose File, Save to save your Word document in a Word format before saving it in an HTML file format. Then, you can make changes to your Word document later.)

When you are finished working with a document, you should close the file to free up valuable RAM. To close a document window, simply click the Close button (☒) in the upper right-hand corner of the document window. When the document window is maximized, its Close button appears on the right side of the Menu bar. Let's close the "Practice Paragraph" document file.

Perform the following steps . . .

1. CLICK: Close button (☒) of the document window
    (*CAUTION:* If you click the Close button for the application window, Word will close.)
2. If other documents appear in the document area, repeat step 1 to clear them from memory.

BEGINNING A NEW DOCUMENT

When Word is first loaded, a blank document automatically appears on the screen. If you have already typed information into this document and would now like to work with a new document, you must choose the File, New command or click the New button (🗅) on the Standard toolbar.

Now let's display a new blank document.

Perform the following steps . . .

1. Ensure that there are no open documents in the document area.

2. CLICK: New button (🗅) on the Standard toolbar
    A new document appears.

OPENING AN EXISTING DOCUMENT

Now that your document is stored in this electronic filing cabinet called a disk, how do you retrieve the document for editing? To modify or print an existing document, click the Open button (📂) on the Standard toolbar or choose File, Open from the Menu bar. Once the Open dialog box appears, you select the file's location by clicking in the *Look in* drop-down list box. You then double-click the document name appearing in the file list.

In this section, you open the "Practice Paragraph" document from the Data Files location.

Perform the following steps . . .

1. Make sure you have identified the location for retrieving your Data Files. If you require a diskette, place it into the diskette drive now.

2. To practice using the Open dialog box:
    CLICK: Open button (📂) on the Standard toolbar

3. To view your Data Files:
CLICK: down arrow beside the *Look in* drop-down list box
SELECT: *your Data Files location*
Your screen should now appear similar to Figure 1.14. (*Note:* If your Advantage Files are stored along with your Data Files, additional files will appear in the file list on your computer. Figure 1.14 shows the contents of a hard disk folder named *My Documents.*)

FIGURE 1.14

THE OPEN DIALOG BOX

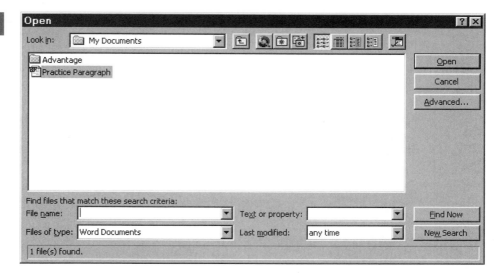

4. To change the display in the Open dialog box, try the following:
CLICK: Detail button (⊞) to see each document's file size and date
CLICK: Properties button (⊞) to see summary information
CLICK: Preview button (⊞) to see a document preview
CLICK: List button (⊞) to see a multiple-column format

5. To open the "Practice Paragraph" document:
DOUBLE-CLICK: Practice Paragraph
The document is loaded into Word's document window.

QUICK REFERENCE
Opening a Document

1. **CLICK: Open button (⊞), or**
   CHOOSE: File, Open from the Menu bar

2. **CLICK: down arrow beside the *Look in* drop-down list box**

3. **SELECT: a file location**

4. **DOUBLE-CLICK: the desired document**

IN ADDITION OPENING A DOCUMENT FROM THE WINDOWS DESKTOP

From the Windows desktop, you can open a document that you've worked with recently. Click the Start button on the taskbar and then choose the Documents command. Then, choose the document's name. The application you used to create the document loads automatically.

IN ADDITION OPEN AN INTERNET DOCUMENT

If your computer has an Internet connection, you can open documents on the World Wide Web or at an FTP site directly from the Open dialog box. In the Open dialog box, you click the Search the Web button (🔍) to launch your Web browser program. Using the procedure specific to your browser, you type in a *URL* (*Uniform Re-source Locator*), an address that points to a specific location on the Internet. All Web URLs begin with "http://". All FTP URLs begin with "ftp://". For more information about opening Internet documents, choose Help, Contents and Index from the Menu bar. Then select the Index tab and type **opening documents on the Internet.**

PRINTING A DOCUMENT

Now that you've learned how to create a document, you will learn how to send it to the printer. This section provides only a brief glimpse at the tools available. A more detailed discussion on printing appears in Session 4.

The quickest method for sending the active document to the printer is to click the Print button (🖨) on the Standard toolbar. When you click this button, no dialog boxes appear asking you to confirm your choice, so ensure that the printer is online and has sufficient paper. You may want to save a few trees by previewing the document on-screen first using the Print Preview button (🔍). You can always click the Print button (🖨) from the Print Preview screen if you want to send the document to the printer.

Now you will print a document.

Perform the following steps . . .

1. Ensure that the "Practice Paragraph" document appears in the document window.

2. To display a preview of how the "Practice Paragraph" document will appear when printed:
   CLICK: Print Preview button (🔍)
   Your screen should now appear similar to Figure 1.15. This view provides an overall picture of the document's layout.

3. At this point it's hard to decipher any of the text. To zoom in a bit further:
   CLICK: down arrow in the Zoom box (29% ▾)
   SELECT: 50% from the drop-down menu

FIGURE 1.15

PRINT PREVIEW

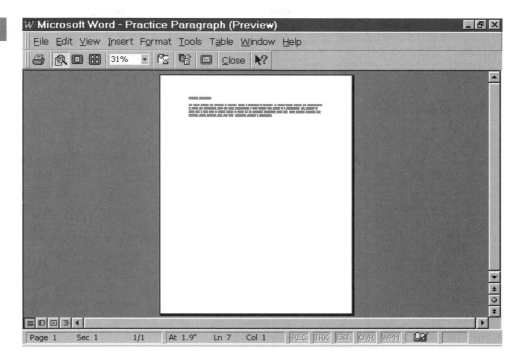

4. Assuming that you are pleased with the Print Preview results:
CLICK: Print button (🖨)
The "Practice Paragraph" document will print to your default printer.

5. Close the "Practice Paragraph" document.

QUICK REFERENCE
Quick Printing

1. **CLICK: Print Preview button (🔍) to see a preview of your document**
2. **CLICK: Print button (🖨) to send your document to the printer**

LEAVING WORD

When you are finished using Word, save your work and exit the program by clicking the Close button (✕) or by choosing the File, Exit command. If you have made
modifications to the active document and have not saved the changes, Word asks
whether the document should be saved or abandoned before exiting the program.

Perform the following steps . . .

1. To exit Word:
CLICK: Close button (✕) of the application window
Assuming that no changes were made to the document, the application is
closed and you are returned to the Windows desktop.

2. To exit Windows:
CHOOSE: Start, Shut Down
SELECT: *Shutdown the computer?* option button
CLICK: Yes command button

QUICK REFERENCE	● **CLICK: Close button ([X]) of the application window, or**
Exiting Word	● **CHOOSE: File, Exit**

SUMMARY

We began by introducing Microsoft Office 97 and describing the most notable features of Microsoft Word 97. After loading Microsoft Windows and Word, you were led on a guided tour of the program's major components. We also used the Help facility to retrieve information on menu commands, toolbar buttons, and general procedures.

In the latter half of the session, you created a practice document using the Insert and Overtype modes. You learned how to remove characters using **DELETE** and **BACKSPACE** and how to enter blank lines using **ENTER**. In addition, you learned about Word's automatic spelling and grammar feature. The session finished with discussions on saving, closing, opening, and printing document files. Many of the commands and procedures appearing in this session are provided in the command summary in Table 1.3.

TABLE 1.3	*Task Description*	*Menu Command*	*Toolbar Button*	*Keyboard Shortcut*
Command Summary	Create a new document file	File, New	▯	**CTRL** +n
	Open an existing document file	File, Open	▱	**CTRL** +o
	Close a document file	File, Close		
	Save a document to the disk	File, Save	▤	**CTRL** +s
	Preview a document for printing	File, Print Preview	▨	
	Print a document	File, Print	▨	**CTRL** +p
	Save a document to the disk, specifying the filename	File, Save As		
	Leave Word	File, Exit	✕	
	Reverse the last command(s) executed	Edit, Undo	↺▾	**CTRL** +z
	Access the Word Help facility	Help, Contents and Index		
	Access the Office Assistant	Help, Microsoft Word Help	▨	**F1**

KEY TERMS

application window

In Microsoft Windows, each running application program appears in its own application window. These windows can be sized and moved anywhere on the Windows desktop.

document window

In Microsoft Windows, each open document appears in its own document window. These windows can be sized and moved anywhere within the document area.

End of Document Marker

The black, horizontal bar that appears at the end of a Word document. You cannot move the insertion point beyond this marker.

grammar checker

In word processing programs, a program that checks the grammar and word usage in a document.

hyperlinks

These are highlighted words or phrases that appear when viewing information on the World Wide Web. You click the hyperlink to view a different document.

insertion point

The vertical flashing bar in Word that indicates your current position in the document. The insertion point shows where the next typed characters will appear.

Internet

A collection of computer networks that spans the globe.

Intranet

A local or wide area network that uses Internet technologies to share information.

mail merge

A procedure that typically involves combining data that is stored in a data file with a form letter created in a word processing software program.

spelling checker

In word processing programs, a program that checks the spelling of words in a document.

thesaurus

In word processing programs, a program that provides a list of synonyms and antonyms for a selected word.

Undo command

In a software application, a command that reverses the last command executed.

URL

Standing for *Uniform Resource Locator*, a name given to an address or location on the Internet.

word processing

Preparation of a document using a microcomputer.

word wrap

When the insertion point reaches the right-hand margin of a line, it automatically wraps to the left margin of the next line; the user does not have to press **ENTER** at the end of each line.

World Wide Web

A visual interface for the Internet.

EXERCISES

SHORT ANSWER

1. What is the purpose of the Office Assistant?

2. What Internet features are included in Office 97?

3. What are the four levels of formatting in a document?

4. What are some examples of mail merge activities?

5. Why is it significant to know that the default mode in Word is the Insert mode?

6. Why is it important to close a document before retrieving another file?

7. What happens if you press **ENTER** when the insertion point is in the middle of a paragraph?

8. How do you delete a single character to the left of the insertion point?

9. What can you do to remove the red wavy underlines from a document?

10. What is the difference between the File, Save and File, Save As commands?

HANDS-ON

(*Note*: Ensure that you know the location of your Advantage Files and where to store your Data Files. If necessary, ask your instructor or lab assistant for additional information.)

1. Create the document pictured in Figure 1.16.

FIGURE 1.16

"MOVING
ANNOUNCEMENT"
DOCUMENT

> WE'RE MOVING TO SPAIN on May 15, 1997!
>
> Our new address and phone are:
>
>   Calle Blanca de Rivera, 19
>   28010 Madrid, Spain
>   Local Phone: 311-0001
>
> ADIOS!

 a. Save the document as "Moving Announcement" to your Data Files location.

 b. Close the "Moving Announcement" document.

 c. Retrieve the "Moving Announcement" document from the Data Files location and insert the following text after the first sentence: Please come visit us!

 d. Save the "Moving Announcement" document to your Data Files location once again.

 e. Print and then close the document.

2. Pretend you're having a garage sale. Open the "Garage" document from the Advantage Files location and edit it to include the date March 16, 1997; the time 10 A.M. to 12 P.M.; and your address. When finished, save it to the Data Files location as "Garage Sale." (*Hint*: If your Data Files location is different from your Advantage Files location, you will need to choose File, Save As from the Menu bar to choose a different disk location.) Close the "Garage Sale" document.

3. Create the document appearing in Figure 1.17. Make sure you include your name and job title (real or imaginary) in the closing of the letter. Save this document to the Data Files location as "Al Martino."

FIGURE 1.17

"AL MARTINO"
DOCUMENT

September 24, 1997

Mr. Al Martino
210 Spruce Way
Stanford, CA 94305

Dear Mr. Martino:

Thank you for your letter regarding the upcoming
event. I am in complete agreement with you that the
number of persons attending must be limited to 200.
Your idea of having this event catered sounds
fantastic!

Moving to a different subject, I noticed that the
letter you wrote me was typed using a typewriter.
(You certainly make use of correction fluid!) With
the number of letters you write, you really should
consider purchasing a microcomputer and word
processing software program.

If you are interested, come over to my office and
I'll show you some word processing fundamentals. We
could even use my computer to design and print the
invitations for the event.

Best regards,

Your name

a. Insert the following text between the second and third paragraphs:

    Specifically, word processing software makes it
    easier to change a document by allowing you to do the
    following:

    1. Insert text
    2. Delete text
    3. Move text
    4. Copy text

b. In the first line of the last paragraph, delete the words "If you are interested," and start the sentence with "You should."

c. In the second paragraph, replace the phrase "correction fluid" with "white-out" using Overtype mode and the **(DELETE)** key.

d. Save the document back to the Data Files location as "Al Martino," replacing the original version.

e. Print the "Al Martino" document.

f. Close the "Al Martino" document.

g. Open a new document.

4. Create the document appearing in Figure 1.18. Make sure you include your name in the closing of the letter. Save this document to the Data Files location as "ABC Realty."

FIGURE 1.18

"ABC REALTY"
DOCUMENT

June 28, 1997

Mr. S. Luis Obispo
Manager, Sales
ABC Realty Inc.
1388 Primrose Lane
Albany, GA 31705

Dear Luis:

Per our conversation yesterday, please accept this letter as confirmation for your order of computer equipment, deliverable next week.

As discussed, five computers will be installed: one at reception, two for sales, one for accounting, and the last one for yourself. We will also be installing DOS 3.3 and WordPerfect 5.1 at that time.

Training on these software programs will begin the week after installation, per the schedule arranged in our conversation. By the way, I've included the cost for training in the total cost of the equipment.

If I can be of further assistance or if you have any questions, please do not hesitate to contact me.

Yours sincerely,
Tech Talk Technology

Your name
Accounts Representative

a. In the second paragraph, perform the following editing changes:

Text Before Editing	Text After Editing
DOS 3.3	Windows
WordPerfect 5.1	Microsoft Word 97
at that time	the next morning

b. Remove the entire third paragraph, starting with "Training on."

c. Enter the phone number (800) 581-8799 below the last line.

d. Using the Save button (), save the document as "ABC Realty" to the Data Files location.

e. Close the document.

f. Retrieve the "ABC Realty" document from the Data Files location.

g. Edit the phone number to read (800) 588-1799.

h. Save the document once again to the Data Files location.

i. Print and then close the document.

5. On your own, write a letter to a friend. This document should begin with the current date, include at least two paragraphs, and end with your name in the closing. Make sure to correct any spelling or grammar errors. Save the document as "On Your Own-1" to the Data Files location and then print the document. *Extra Credit*: If you don't want anyone besides yourself to be able to open or edit this letter in the future, protect the letter with a password.

6. On your own, explore a Microsoft Word Help topic. Pick a Microsoft Word Help topic that interests you and write about it in a few paragraphs. Make sure to explain why you chose the topic and how to perform the procedures described. (For example, you may be interested in creating indexes.) Insert your name and the current date at the beginning of the document. Save the document as "On Your Own-2" to the Data Files location and then print the document.

CASE PROBLEMS   **THE EXPERT HANDYMAN, INC.**

(*Note*: In the following case problems, assume the role of the primary characters and perform the same steps that they identify. You may want to re-read the session opening.)

1. George is determined to use Microsoft Word to create invoices. He has outlined the information by hand (as shown below) that he wants to include on every invoice.

The Expert HandyMan, Inc.
1990 Jillson Street
Irvine, California 92718

Invoice Number:
Date:
Customer Name:
Address:
City, State, Zip:

[Insert a sentence describing the job performed and result.]

[Number of hours] hours at $30 per hour = [Insert total amount due]

We appreciate your business.

Sincerely,

George Perrera
President, The Expert HandyMan, Inc.

Referring to the handwritten notes, create a generic invoice document that George can edit each time he needs to generate a new invoice. When finished, save the document as "Invoice" to the Data Files location. Print "Invoice."

2. Yesterday, George completed a job for Kenneth Richards at 436 Wetlands Way, Irvine, California, 92718. Kenneth's dryer wasn't working properly, and George had to clean the fan unit and replace the main airflow tube. George must now generate an invoice for the two hours spent at Mr. Richards' house. Retrieve the blank invoice stored in the Data Files location, edit the invoice to reflect Mr. Richards' information, add the Invoice Number GP-946, and then save the document as "Invoice - Kenneth Richards" to the Data Files location.

3. George feels so confident with his new word processing skills that he decides to tackle a proposal using Word. In a conversation with a friend, George heard that Isabel Perez at the Holiday Retreat Hotel is looking for someone to spend five days performing odd jobs around the hotel. The problems include doors that won't close properly, locks that stick, faucets that leak, and tables that wobble.

George wants the business at the Holiday Retreat Hotel. He decides to prepare a written proposal stating his hourly wage and describing some of his accomplishments, including the job he just completed for Kenneth Richards. The Holiday Retreat Hotel is located at 2987 W. Howard Street, Irvine, California, 92718. Prepare a proposal document for George and save it as "Proposal - Holiday Retreat Hotel" to the Data Files location. Print the document.

4. George has decided to put an advertisement in the local paper for The Expert HandyMan, complete with his address, phone number, and his new slogan: "We can fix anything that needs fixing!" He wants the ad to run for the next month in the Business Classifieds section of the weekend edition. Two hours after calling the local paper for information on submitting an ad, George receives a message on his answering machine. The message is from Rachel Yenkel, the advertising manager.

    Hi, Mr. Perrera. Please send me the text for your advertisement. Insert the words "BEGIN TEXT" one line above the text of your advertisement and "END TEXT" one line below. Send the ad text in a letter to my attention at 4910 S. Commerce Street, Irvine, California, 92718. Also, you will have to let me know what section you want the ad to appear in and how many days you want the ad to run. Bye.

    When you have created the advertisement, save the document to the Data Files location as "Local Advertisement." Print the advertisement.

Microsoft Word 97 for Windows

Character and Paragraph Formatting

SESSION

2

IRWIN

COMPUTER & INFORMATION TECHNOLOGY

SESSION OUTLINE

INTRODUCTION

Word processing programs make assumptions about how a document should appear when printed. For most business documents, these assumptions or default settings work well. However, you may also want to tailor a document to meet a specific need. This session teaches you how to use Word's formatting commands to enhance your work.

| CASE STUDY | ADVANCED SOFTWARE DESIGN, INC. |

Advanced Software Design, Inc. (ASD) is a software development company that specializes in writing Windows-based software applications. Upon request, ASD submits a proposal to a company or individual who expresses a need for a custom-written application. For example, Harry Zidell of Business Assistance Services, an employment agency, recently contracted with ASD to build a performance evaluation program for testing his candidates. A few days after talking to Alethia Montera, a consultant at ASD, Harry received a proposal in the mail. The proposal looked fair, and the project is now underway.

While speaking to a client on the phone or in person, Alethia takes handwritten notes outlining the client's needs. After the conversation or meeting, she estimates the number of hours required to complete the project and calculates the cost of the job. She then sends her notes to Mary, who types them up using Microsoft Word and returns them to Alethia for final review. Mary likes working for Alethia and hopes that one day she can work side-by-side with her in assessing clients' needs. To show her initiative and desire for advancement, Mary decides to improve the look of ASD's proposals using Word's formatting commands. But where to begin? Mary has never tried to format a document using Word.

In this session, you and Mary learn more about Word's default settings and how they affect your documents, how to select text, and how to format characters and paragraphs.

WORD'S DEFAULT SETTINGS

While the words in a document contain the message, a formatted document can better communicate that message. Not only does formatting let you add your own personality to your work, it also improves a document's readability. With proper formatting, you can direct readers' attention to important concepts, improve overall comprehension of the material, and better the reader's chance of recalling the material. And last, it can look really nice!

You begin this session by learning how to change Word's formatting assumptions or default settings. These settings affect how your documents appear on the screen and how they look when printed. This session teaches you Word's most commonly used character and paragraph formatting commands. With these commands, you can produce professional-looking resumes, letters, and reports with minimal effort.

When you first load Word or click the New button ([D]) on the Standard toolbar, a new document appears based upon Word's Normal template. This template provides a set of basic formatting assumptions about your new document, including paper size, margin widths, and default font. You can modify these initial assumptions directly in the template or you can start with a new document based on the template and customize the settings later. The **default settings** for a new document based on the Normal template are listed in Table 2.1.

TABLE 2.1	Option	Setting
Settings for the Normal template	Paper Size	8.5 inches wide by 11 inches tall
	Top and Bottom Margins	1 inch
	Left and Right Margins	1.25 inches
	Page Numbering	None
	Line Spacing	Single space
	Font (Typeface)	Times New Roman
	Font Size	10 point
	Tabs	Every 0.5 inch
	Justification	Left-justified with a ragged right margin

In this section you practice modifying the default page layout options.

Perform the following steps . . .

1. Make sure that you have identified the location for retrieving your Advantage Files and for saving your Data Files. If you require a diskette, place it in the diskette drive now.

2. A new document should appear in the Word application window. [*Hint*: If a document currently appears on your screen, close it by clicking its Close button (☒) and then click the New button (▯) on the Standard toolbar.]

3. To view the default page layout settings for this new document:
CHOOSE: File, Page Setup
CLICK: *Margins* tab
Your screen should now appear similar to Figure 2.1. Notice that there are four tabs along the top of this dialog box: Margins, Paper Size, Paper Source, and Layout.

FIGURE 2.1

PAGE SETUP
DIALOG BOX:
MARGINS TAB

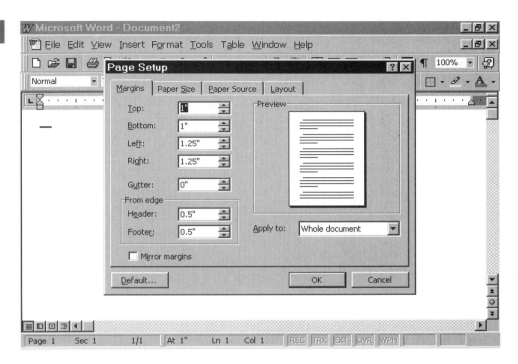

4. To increase and decrease the values for the margin settings, you click the up and down triangular-shaped increment buttons, sometimes called *Spin box controls*, positioned to the right of each text box. Let's increase the top margin to 1.5 inches:
CLICK: up increment button until 1.5 appears in the *Top* text box
The *Preview* area immediately shows the increase in the top margin. (*Note*: The margin settings increase in increments of .1 of an inch on each click. You can also type a number into the text box to enter a more detailed measurement.)

5. To ensure that you are using letter-size paper:
CLICK: *Paper Size* tab
Your screen should now appear similar to Figure 2.2. As you can see in this figure, the default paper size is Letter with a Portrait orientation.

FIGURE 2.2

PAGE SETUP
DIALOG BOX:
PAPER SIZE TAB

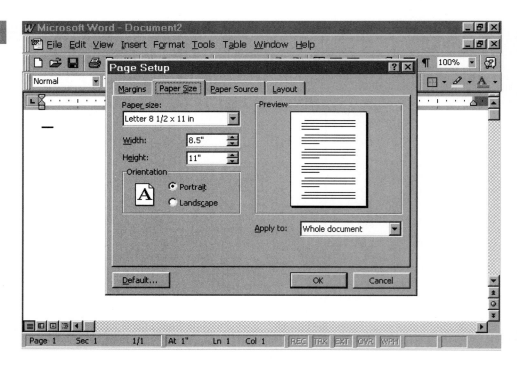

6. To return to the document:
PRESS: ⎡ENTER⎤ or CLICK: OK
The document now has a 1.5-inch top margin.

For now, we're finished looking at the default page layout options. In the next few sections, you learn how to move efficiently through a document and to block text using the mouse and keyboard. These skills are important in learning how to select text and issue character and paragraph formatting commands.

Moving through a document

Before inserting or editing text in a document, you must position the insertion point using the mouse or keyboard. Like many procedures in Word, the mouse provides the easiest method for navigating through a document. To position the insertion point, you scroll the document window until the desired text appears and then click the I-beam mouse pointer in the text. Contrary to what you might think, scrolling the document window does not automatically move the insertion point! If you forget to click the mouse and start typing or press an arrow key, Word takes you back to the original location of the insertion point before you started scrolling.

Common methods for scrolling the document window are provided below:

To scroll the window . . .	Do this . . .
One line at a time	Click the up (▲) and down (▼) arrowheads on the vertical scroll bar.
One screen at a time	Click the vertical scroll bar itself, above and below the scroll box (▢).
One page at a time	Click on these scroll bar symbols to move to the previous page (⬆) or to the next page (⬇) in a document.
Pages at a time	Drag the scroll box (▢) along the vertical scroll bar.

In addition to the above methods, you can select to browse through a specific type of object using the Select Browse Object button (◉) on the vertical scroll bar. When used in conjunction with the Next Page and Previous Page buttons you can browse through specific types of objects such as endnotes, footnotes, headings, sections, graphics, or tables.

Although not as intuitive as using the mouse, there are several keyboard shortcuts for moving the insertion point through a document. If you are a touch-typist, you may prefer these methods over using a mouse. Table 2.2 provides a summary of the more popular keystrokes.

TABLE 2.2	Key	Description
Using the keyboard to move the Insertion Point	⬆ or ⬇	Moves up or down one line
	CTRL + ⬆	Moves to the previous paragraph
	CTRL + ⬇	Moves to the next paragraph
	⬅ or ➡	Moves to the previous or next character
	CTRL + ⬅	Moves to the beginning of the previous word
	CTRL + ➡	Moves to the beginning of the next word
	PgUp or PgDn	Moves up or down one screen
	HOME or END	Moves to the beginning or end of the current line
	CTRL + HOME	Moves to the beginning of the document
	CTRL + END	Moves to the end of the document
	F5 (GoTo)	Moves to a specific line, section, or page number
	SHIFT + F5 (GoBack)	Moves to the last three areas, in order, that you have edited in a document

In this section you practice moving through a document.

Perform the following steps . . .

1. To display your Advantage Files:
   CLICK: Open button ( ) on the Standard toolbar
   CLICK: down arrow beside the *Look in* drop-down list box
   SELECT: *your Advantage Files location*

2. To retrieve the "Ethics" document:
   DOUBLE-CLICK: "Ethics" in the file area
   Your screen should now appear similar to Figure 2.3.

FIGURE 2.3

THE "ETHICS" DOCUMENT

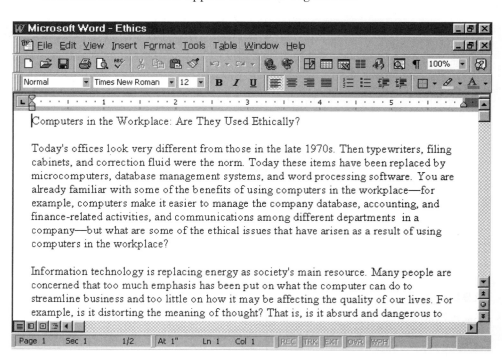

3. To move down through the document one screen at a time:
   CLICK: below the scroll box on the vertical scroll bar repeatedly

4. To move to the top of the document:
   DRAG: the scroll box to the top of the vertical scroll bar
   Notice that as you drag the scroll box along the scroll bar, Word displays the current page number.

5. To move to the bottom of the document using the keyboard:
   PRESS: CTRL + END

6. To move back to the top of the document using the keyboard:
   PRESS: CTRL + HOME

7. To move to the end of the current line:
   PRESS: END

8. To move to the beginning of the current line:
   PRESS: HOME

9. To move to the top of the second page in the document:
CLICK: Next Page button (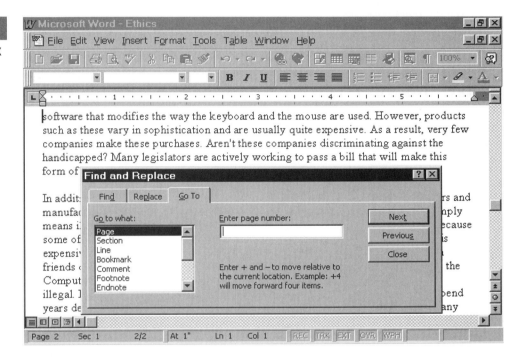) on the vertical scroll bar
The insertion point automatically moves to the first line of page 2.

10. To practice using the Go To dialog box:
DOUBLE-CLICK: on the page area ("Page 2") in the Status bar
Your screen should now appear similar to Figure 2.4.

FIGURE 2.4

THE GO TO DIALOG BOX

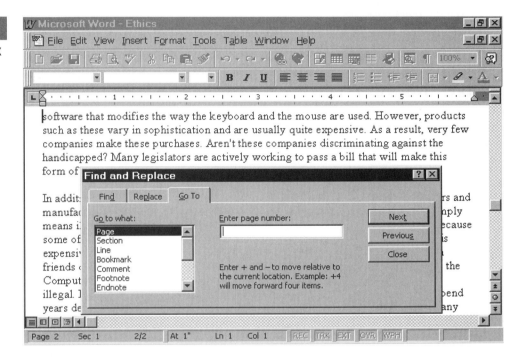

11. TYPE: P1L8
CLICK: Go To button or PRESS: ENTER
CLICK: Close command button
The "P" tells Word that the following number is a page number, and the "L" tells Word that the next number is a line number. The letters can be typed in either uppercase or lowercase characters. In this step, the insertion point is moved to line 8 on page 1.

12. To move to the top of the document:
PRESS: CTRL + HOME

QUICK REFERENCE
Accessing the
Go To Dialog Box

- **DOUBLE-CLICK: on the page area in the Status bar, or**
- **PRESS: F5 (Go To), or**
- **PRESS: CTRL +g, or**
- **CHOOSE: Edit, Go To**

IN ADDITION MARKING LOCATIONS WITH BOOKMARKS

You can also name locations, called *bookmarks,* in your document and then use the Go To dialog box when you want to move to them quickly.

To create a bookmark, position the cursor at the location you want to name and then choose Insert,

Bookmark from the Menu bar. Type a name for th-bookmark (up to 40 characters) and then click the Add button.

To move to a bookmark, display the Go To dialog box, select Bookmark from the *Go to what* list box, and then select the bookmark's name from the *Enter bookmark name* drop-down list box.

SELECTING TEXT

Once text has been typed into a document, you make formatting changes by first selecting the text and then issuing the appropriate command. Selected text always appears highlighted in reverse video (white text on a black background). A selection may include letters, words, lines, paragraphs, or even the entire document. When you finish formatting a selection, press an arrow key or click anywhere in the document to remove the highlighting from the text.

BLOCKING TEXT

Word provides an invisible column in the extreme left margin of the document window called the **Selection bar.** When the mouse is moved into this area, the pointer changes from an I-beam to a right-pointing diagonal arrow (⚐). The Selection bar provides shortcut methods for selecting text using the mouse, as summarized in Table 2.3 along with other selection methods.

TABLE 2.3	*To select this . . .*	*Do this . . .*
Selecting text using the Mouse	Single Letter	Position the I-beam pointer to the left of the letter you want to select. Press down and hold the left mouse button as you drag the mouse pointer to the right.
	Single Word	Position the I-beam pointer on the word and double-click the left mouse button.
	Single Sentence	Hold down CTRL and click once with the I-beam pointer positioned on any word in the sentence.
	Block of Text	Move the insertion point to the beginning of the block of text and then position the I-beam pointer at the end of the block. Hold down SHIFT and click once.
	Single Line	Move the mouse pointer into the Selection bar, beside the line to be selected. Wait until the pointer changes to a right-pointing arrow and then click once.
	Single Paragraph	Move the mouse pointer into the Selection bar, beside the paragraph to be selected. Wait until the pointer changes to a right-pointing arrow and then double-click. You can also triple-click with the I-beam mouse pointer positioned inside a paragraph.
	Entire Document	Move the mouse pointer into the Selection bar. Wait until the pointer changes to a right-pointing arrow and then hold down CTRL and click once. You can also triple-click with the I-beam mouse pointer positioned in the Selection bar.

Next you practice selecting text using the "Ethics" document.

Perform the following steps . . .

1. To select the word "Computers" in the title, first position the I-beam mouse pointer on the word.

2. DOUBLE-CLICK: Computers
   The word and its trailing space should be highlighted in reverse video.

3. To select the letters "Work" in the word "Workplace," you must first position the I-beam pointer to the left of the "W" in "Workplace."

4. PRESS: left mouse button and hold it down
   DRAG: I-beam to the right until Work is highlighted

5. To select the first sentence in the first paragraph below the title, first position the I-beam pointer on the word "offices." (*Note:* The mouse pointer can be placed over any word in the sentence.)

6. PRESS: CTRL and hold it down
   CLICK: left mouse button once
   The first sentence, including the period and spaces, are highlighted.

7. To select only the third line in the first paragraph, position the mouse pointer to the left of the line in the Selection bar. The mouse pointer should change from an I-beam to a right-pointing diagonal arrow.

8. CLICK: the Selection bar beside the third line

9. To select the entire first paragraph:
DOUBLE-CLICK: the Selection bar beside the first paragraph
(*Note*: You can also position the I-beam pointer on any word in the paragraph and triple-click the left mouse button to select the entire paragraph.)

10. To select the entire document:
PRESS: [CTRL] and hold it down
CLICK: once anywhere in the Selection bar
(*Note*: You can also position the mouse pointer in the Selection bar and triple-click the left mouse button to select the entire document.)

11. To remove highlighting from the text:
CLICK: once anywhere in the text area

12. To return to the top of the document:
PRESS: [CTRL] + [HOME]

To select text using the keyboard, you can use any combination of the keyboard shortcuts for moving the insertion point around the document while holding down the [SHIFT] key. Most people, however, find that the mouse methods provide all the flexibility they need for selecting blocks of text.

DELETING BLOCKS OF TEXT

Previously, you were told to delete text one character at a time using the [BACKSPACE] and [DELETE] keys. However, the ability to select characters, paragraphs, and documents allows you to delete larger blocks of text easily. Now you will practice deleting and replacing text in a document.

Perform the following steps . . .

1. To select the phrase in the title that reads "Are They Used Ethically?" first position the I-beam pointer to the left of the word "Are."

2. PRESS: left mouse button and hold it down
DRAG: I-beam to the right until the question mark is highlighted
(*Note*: If you select the space following the question mark, the next line will be deleted too.)

3. To remove this phrase from the title:
PRESS: [DELETE]

4. Move the I-beam pointer on the word "Computers" in the title:
DOUBLE-CLICK: Computers
The word is selected.

5. TYPE: Technology
Rather than using the Overtype mode, you can select the text to be replaced and then type in the new information. The typing automatically replaces the text selection.

6. To Undo this last editing change:
    CLICK: Undo button (⟲▾) in the Standard toolbar
    The word "Computers" reappears.

7. To demonstrate a basic formatting command, let's change the capitalization
    of the selected word "Computers":
    CHOOSE: Format, Change Case
    SELECT: UPPERCASE
    PRESS: ENTER or CLICK: OK
    The word changes from "Computers" to "COMPUTERS." (*Note*: You can
    also use SHIFT + F3 to toggle the selected text between uppercase, lower-
    case, and initial caps.)

8. Close the document window without saving the changes:
    CLICK: Close button (✕) of the document window
    CLICK: No command button

Now that you know how to move through documents and select text, formatting
your documents will be much easier. The next section begins with an introduction
to the character formatting commands.

CHARACTER FORMATTING COMMANDS

In word processing software, enhancing the appearance of text is referred to as
character formatting. Specifically, character formatting involves selecting typefaces, font sizes, and attributes for text. Some of the attributes available in Word
include bold, italic, underline, highlight, font color, strikethrough, shadow, outline,
superscript, and subscript. You can even add animated effects, such as a blinking
background or a shimmer, to text. Although these enhancement features are effective in drawing the reader's attention, they can also detract from the message you
are trying to communicate. Most publishing professionals advocate using no more
than four typefaces or fonts in a document. Still, there is no better gauge than
common sense and good taste.

Word's character formatting commands are accessed through the Font dialog box
(Figure 2.5), the Formatting toolbar, or by using shortcut keyboard combinations.
Since many of the features are accessible from the Formatting toolbar and shortcut keys, you may never need to use the Format, Font menu command except to
see a preview of a desired font or other attribute in the dialog box. Table 2.4 summarizes the mouse and keyboard methods for choosing character formatting commands.

FIGURE 2.5

FONT DIALOG BOX

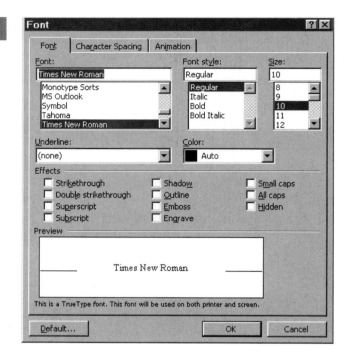

TABLE 2.4	Toolbar Button	Keyboard Shortcut	Description
Character Formatting Summary	**B**	CTRL + b	Makes the selected text **bold**
	I	CTRL + i	*Italicizes* the selected text
	U	CTRL + u	Applies a <u>single underline</u>
		CTRL + SHIFT + d	Applies a <u>double underline</u>
		CTRL + SHIFT + w	Applies underlining to <u>words</u> <u>only</u>
	✎ ▾		Applies color highlighting to text
	A ▾		Changes the font color
	Times New Roman ▾	CTRL + SHIFT + f	Specifies a font or typeface
		CTRL + [	Decrease the point size by 1 point
		CTRL +]	Increase the point size by 1 point
	10 ▾	CTRL + SHIFT + p	Specifies a point size for the font
		CTRL + SHIFT + a	CAPITALIZES the selection
		CTRL + SHIFT + k	Applies SMALL CAPS

TABLE 2.4 *Continued*	*Toolbar Button*	*Keyboard Shortcut*	*Description*
		CTRL + F3	Changes the case of the selection
		CTRL + =	Applies a $_{sub}$script style
		CTRL + SHIFT + =	Applies a ^{super}script style
		CTRL + Space Bar	Removes all character formatting

BOLDFACE, ITALIC, AND UNDERLINES

In Word, you can apply character formatting commands as you type or after you have selected text. In this section you apply boldface, italic, and underlines to the "Ethics" document.

Perform the following steps . . .

1. Retrieve the "Ethics" document from the Advantage Files location. (*Note:* The last four documents that you opened are listed at the bottom of the File pull-down menu. Choose "Ethics" from this list.)

2. To insert a new line between the title and the first paragraph:
   PRESS: END
   PRESS: ENTER

3. To add an italicized subtitle for this document:
   CLICK: Italic button (*I*) on the Formatting toolbar
   TYPE: The Information Age and the Age of Humanity

4. To stop typing in italic:
   CLICK: Italic button (*I*)

5. To select this subtitle, position the mouse pointer in the Selection bar to the left of the line and click the left mouse button once.

6. Make the subtitle bold and underlined using the buttons on the Formatting toolbar:
   CLICK: Bold button (**B**)
   CLICK: Underline button (U)

7. To better see the changes you've made:
   CLICK: anywhere in the text area

8. Make the following formatting changes in the first paragraph using either the Formatting toolbar buttons or the keyboard shortcuts.

Text to be formatted	Formatting to apply
microcomputers	italic and bold
database management system	italic
word processing software	italic
ethical issues	word underline only

QUICK REFERENCE
Boldface, Italic, and
Underlines

- To make text bold, click the Bold button (**B**) or press (CTRL) + b
- To italicize text, click the Italic button (*I*) or press (CTRL) + i
- To underline text, click the Underline button (U) or press (CTRL) + u

TYPEFACES, FONTS, AND POINT SIZES

One of the more interesting character formatting options is the ability to select from a variety of typefaces. A **typeface** is a style of print. A **font** is defined as all the symbols and characters of a particular typeface for a given point size. Many DOS word processing programs do not utilize a variety of fonts, unless they are available through an individual software vendor or resident in the printer's memory. Microsoft Windows, on the other hand, provides easy access to several popular typefaces.

The font and point size can be changed before typing new text or after selecting text. Although you can use the Font dialog box to set the font and point size, it is easier to use the drop-down lists on the Formatting toolbar. In this section you change some of the fonts and point sizes in the "Ethics" document.

Perform the following steps . . .

1. SELECT: the main title on the first line

2. To display a list of the available fonts:
   CLICK: down arrow beside the *Font* drop-down list (Times New Roman ▼)

3. Scroll through the font choices by clicking the up and down arrows on the drop-down list's scroll bar or by dragging the scroll box.

4. SELECT: Arial (or a font that is available on your computer)
   (*Hint*: You select a font from the drop-down list by clicking on it.)

5. To display the range of available font sizes:
   CLICK: down arrow beside the *Font Size* drop-down list (10 ▼)

6. SELECT: 16-point font size
   CLICK: Bold button (**B**)
   PRESS: (HOME) to remove the highlighting
   Your screen should now appear similar to Figure 2.6.

FIGURE 2.6

THE "ETHICS" DOCUMENT
AFTER CHARACTER
FORMATTING

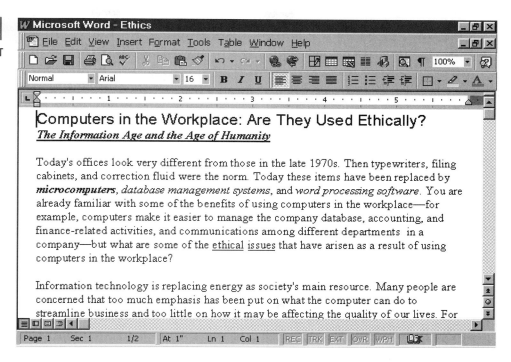

QUICK REFERENCE

QUICK REFERENCE
Typefaces, Fonts,
and Point Sizes

- **To select a typeface, click the *Fonts* drop-down list (Times Roman) in the Formatting toolbar and then click on the desired font.**
- **To change the font size, click the *Font Size* drop-down list (10) in the Formatting toolbar and then click on the desired point size.**

HIGHLIGHT, COLOR, AND ANIMATION

A number of features exist for enhancing how a document appears on the screen. These features are especially useful when others will be reviewing your document online and you want to draw attention to certain elements. In this section, we describe how to highlight text and add color and animation to a document. You highlight and add color to text using the Highlight (🖉▾) and Font Color (△▾) buttons on the Formatting toolbar. You add animation using the Font dialog box.

In this section you practice highlighting text and adding color and animation to a document.

Perform the following steps . . .

1. To highlight the first sentence:
   SELECT: the first sentence

2. CLICK: Highlight button (🖉▾)
   (*Note*: Make sure that you click the left side of the button and not the down arrow.) The sentence should be highlighted in yellow, or in the currently selected color. Your screen should now appear similar to Figure 2.7.

FIGURE 2.7

HIGHLIGHTING TEXT

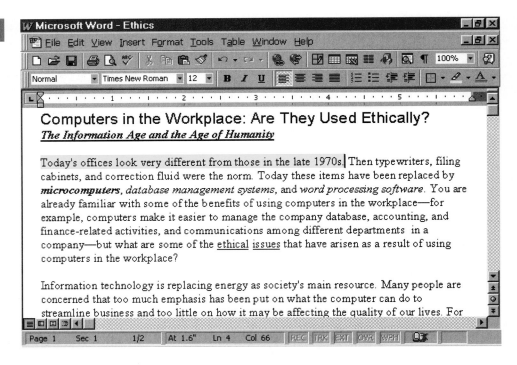

3. To remove the text highlight:
   SELECT: the first sentence
   CLICK: down arrow in the Highlight button (🖊▾)
   SELECT: None
   The text is no longer highlighted. (*Note*: Before you can highlight text in the future, you will have to re-select a color option using the Highlight button.)

4. Let's try adding color to the first paragraph.
   SELECT: the first paragraph
   CLICK: Font Color button (▲▾)
   (*Note*: Make sure that you click the left side of the button and not the down arrow.)
   CLICK: in the document window to remove the highlighting
   The paragraph text should now appear red, or in the currently selected color. Your screen should now appear similar to Figure 2.8.

FIGURE 2.8

COLORING TEXT

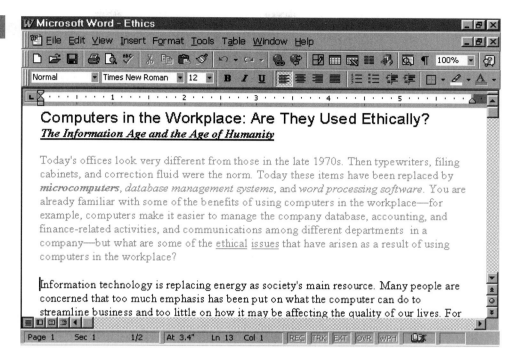

5. To select a new color, you click the down arrow in the Font Color button ([⬛ ▼]). On your own, color the first paragraph blue.

6. Now let's try animating the subtitle of the document. To do this, you will use the *Animation* tab in the Font dialog box.
SELECT: the main title (1st line) at the top of the document

7. CHOOSE: Format, Font
CLICK: *Animation* tab

8. Experiment with the different effects by clicking them in the Animations list box. Before continuing:
CLICK: Sparkle Text
PRESS: **ENTER** or CLICK: OK

9. To save the file to your Data Files location:
CHOOSE: File, Save As

10. To specify a filename for the document:
TYPE: Ethics-Version 2

11. To specify where the document will be saved, do the following:
CLICK: down arrow beside the *Save in* drop-down list box
SELECT: *your Data Files location*
PRESS: **ENTER** or CLICK: Save command button

12. Print the "Ethics-Version 2" document. (*Note*: Your highlighting and coloring will appear as shades of gray when printing on a black and white printer, and your animated effects only appear on the screen.)

QUICK REFERENCE
Adding Highlighting
and Color

- To add highlighting, click the Highlight button (⟨🖊️▾⟩). To change the highlight color, click the down arrow on the Highlight button and choose None (no color) or another color.
- To color text, click the Font Color button (⟨🅰️▾⟩). To change the color, click the down arrow on the Font Color button and choose Automatic (black) or another color.

QUICK REFERENCE
Animating Text

1. CHOOSE: Format, Font
2. CLICK: *Animation* tab
3. SELECT: an Animation style
   PRESS: ⟨ENTER⟩ or CLICK: OK

USING THE FORMAT PAINTER

Word's Format Painter feature lets you copy character and paragraph formatting from one area in your document to another area. To copy character formatting, you select the text with the desired formatting and click the Format Painter button (⟨📋⟩) on the Standard toolbar. When you move the mouse pointer into the document area, it becomes an I-beam attached to a paintbrush. To apply the formatting, you drag the mouse pointer over the text that you want to format. When you release the mouse button, the formatting characteristics are copied from the original selection to your new selection.

To copy formatting to multiple areas in a document, you double-click the Format Painter button (⟨📋⟩) after selecting the originally formatted text. As described in the previous paragraph, you paint the first selection by dragging the mouse pointer over the desired text. However, this time the paintbrush mouse pointer doesn't disappear when you finish applying the first coat. You continue applying formatting to additional text selections and then click the Format Painter button (⟨📋⟩) when you are done.

In this section you practice using the Format Painter.

Perform the following steps . . .

1. Retrieve a document called "Paint" from the Advantage Files location.
2. SELECT: Features
3. To format the heading:
   CLICK: Bold button (⟨**B**⟩)
   CLICK: Italic button (⟨*I*⟩)
   SELECT: Arial font from the *Font* drop-down list (⟨Times New Roman ▾⟩)
   SELECT: 14-point size from the *Font Size* drop-down list (⟨10 ▾⟩)
   (*Note*: If you don't have the Arial font on your computer, select an alternate font.)
4. To copy the formatting characteristics that you just selected:
   DOUBLE-CLICK: Features
   (*Note*: "Features" may already be selected.)

5. CLICK: Format Painter button ()

6. Move the mouse pointer into the document area. Notice that it becomes an I-beam attached to a paintbrush.

7. To copy the formatting to the second heading:
DRAG: mouse pointer over the subheading "Future Expectations"
When you release the mouse button, the second heading is formatted with the same characteristics as the first heading.

8. To format "Windows 95" in the first sentence:
SELECT: Windows 95

9. CLICK: Bold button (**B**)
CLICK: Italic button (*I*)

10. To copy this formatting to several areas in the document:
DOUBLE-CLICK: Format Painter button ()

11. Using the I-beam paintbrush mouse pointer, select all occurrences of "Windows 95" and "Windows NT" in the document. (*Tip*: You can double-click words as you would with the regular I-beam mouse pointer to apply the formatting.)

12. To finish using the paintbrush mouse pointer:
CLICK: Format Painter button ()

13. Save the document as "Painted" to your Data Files location. (*Remember*: You must use the Save As command if your Data Files are stored in a different location from your Advantage Files.)

14. Close the document.

QUICK REFERENCE
Using the Format Painter Button ()

1. SELECT: the text with the desired formatting characteristics
2. CLICK: Format Painter button ()
3. SELECT: the text that you want to format

IN ADDITION FORMATTING CHARACTERS WITH STYLES

A *character style* is a set of formats that can contain any specification found in the Font dialog box (Figure 2.5), such as font type, type style, and point size. When you apply a style to a selection of text, all the formatting instructions in the style are executed at once. When you edit a style, any text that conforms to the style is updated immediately.

If you work with documents that contain lots of formatting, styles will (1) save you time, (2) promote consistent formatting throughout your documents, and (3) make it easier for you to edit a document's format.

To find out more about styles, choose Help, Contents and Index. Select the Index tab and then type **styles** to display a list of topics.

IN ADDITION FORMATTING CHARACTERS WITH WORDART

To add special effects to your document text, consider entering or formatting your text using WordArt. WordArt provides a collection of commands for adding special effects, such as a wavy look, to your text.

1.   Position the insertion point where you want to insert text formatted by WordArt, or select existing text that you want to format with WordArt.

2.   CHOOSE: Insert, Picture, WordArt
(*Note:* You can also click the WordArt button on the WordArt toolbar.)

3.   Select a style in the WordArt Gallery dialog box and then press (ENTER) or click OK.

4.   TYPE: the desired text into the Edit WordArt Text dialog box

5.   Format the text using buttons in the Edit WordArt Text dialog box.

6.   When you're finished:
CLICK: OK

7.   Enhance the selected WordArt object using the WordArt toolbar, if necessary.

8.   To resize the object, point to it and click. Selection handles appear around the object. Drag a selection handle in the desired direction. (*Note:* To delete an object, point to it and click. Then press (DELETE).)

PARAGRAPH FORMATTING COMMANDS

Paragraph formatting involves changing indentation, alignment, line spacing, and tab settings for a paragraph. As with character formatting, many paragraph formatting commands are accessible using the mouse or keyboard shortcut combinations. Using a mouse, you can change alignments and indent paragraphs by clicking buttons on the Formatting toolbar or create hanging indents and set tab stops by dragging symbols on the Ruler. For entering specific measurements and accessing the full gamut of paragraph formatting options, choose the Format, Paragraph command to display the dialog box shown in Figure 2.9.

FIGURE 2.9

PARAGRAPH DIALOG BOX

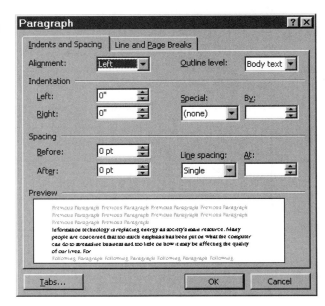

Word stores formatting information in the **Paragraph Symbol** (¶). To apply paragraph formatting commands to a paragraph, position the insertion point anywhere in the paragraph—you do not need to select any text—and then issue the desired command. To remove paragraph formatting, you can press ENTER +q to return to the Normal style. You can also delete the paragraph mark to make the current paragraph assume the formatting characteristics of the subsequent paragraph.

When you first install Word onto your computer, the paragraph marks are hidden from view. To display the paragraph marks and all other hidden symbols, click the Show/Hide button (¶) on the Formatting toolbar. Along with the paragraph marks, Word reveals spaces (as dots), tabs (as right-pointing arrows →), and other formatting codes and symbols. It's very important to note that these are *nonprinting symbols*—they will not show up on the printed page.

A favorite feature in Word is the ability to display a help bubble showing you the formatting characteristics of your text. To display the bubble, choose Help, What's This? from the Menu bar and then click the question mark mouse pointer on the desired text area. A bubble will appear with character and paragraph formatting information. To remove the Help bubble, you press ESC or choose Help, What's This? again.

In this section you display the hidden symbols and formatting information for the "Ethics-Version 2" document.

Perform the following steps . . .

1. Ensure that the "Ethics-Version 2" document appears on your screen.

2. If not already displayed, show all of the hidden symbols in the document by doing the following:
   CLICK: Show/Hide button (¶)
   Paragraph marks (¶) appear in the document wherever the ENTER key was pressed. This view is useful for checking codes and spaces but you may find it distracting.

3. To show the formatting characteristics for the main title:
   CHOOSE: Help, What's This?

4. Position the question mark mouse pointer over any letter in the main title:
   CLICK: left mouse button once
   Your screen should now appear similar to Figure 2.10.

FIGURE 2.10

HELP BUBBLE FOR
SHOWING FORMATTING
CHARACTERISTICS

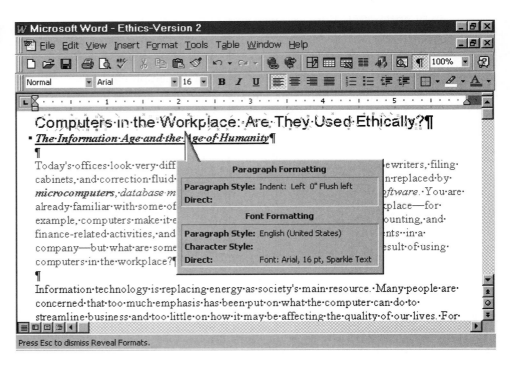

5. To remove the Help bubble:
PRESS: [**ESC**]

6. Before proceeding, let's hide the symbols:
CLICK: Show/Hide button (¶)

INDENTING PARAGRAPHS

Indenting a paragraph means to move a body of text in from the normal page margins. When you indent a paragraph, you temporarily change the text's positioning relative to the left and right margins. You can indent a paragraph on the left side only, right side only, or on both sides (known as a *nested paragraph*).

If you use the Increase Indent (▤) and Decrease Indent (▤) buttons on the Formatting toolbar, indentation is determined by the tab settings in the Ruler. If the tab positions have not been modified, Word assumes you want to use the default 0.5 inch settings. Each time you indent a paragraph, the text moves to the next tab stop. Therefore, to create larger indentations you can set larger gaps between tabs or select the indent command multiple times. You can also customize your indents by dragging the indent markers on the Ruler (shown below).

●   *First-Line Indent Marker*
This indent marker moves only the first line of a paragraph in from the left margin. This paragraph format is often used in letters to avoid having to press the ⟨ **TAB** ⟩ key at the start of each new paragraph.

●   *Left Indent Marker*
The left indent marker moves the body of the entire paragraph in from the left margin.

●   *Right Indent Marker*
The right indent marker moves the body of the entire paragraph in from the right margin. Left and right indents are often used together to set quotations apart from normal body text in a document.

By default, Word positions the first-line and left indent markers on the left margin, and the right indent marker on the right margin. You will now practice changing the paragraph indents using the mouse.

Perform the following steps . . .

1. Ensure that the "Ethics-Version 2" document appears on your screen.

2. Move the insertion point to the second paragraph, starting with the words "Information technology." Position the insertion point to the left of the letter "I" in the word "Information."

3. To add a left indent to this paragraph:
    CLICK: Increase Indent button (⊞)
    The paragraph moves 0.5 inch to the next tab stop. Notice the new location of the indent markers on the Ruler.

4. To view the new settings as they appear in the Paragraph dialog box, position the mouse pointer on the paragraph and click the right mouse button to bring up the shortcut menu.

5. CHOOSE: Paragraph
    The Paragraph dialog box appears. Notice the new value in the *Left Indentation* text box and the sample paragraph in the *Preview* area.

6. To return to the document:
    CLICK: Cancel button

7. To indent the paragraph 1 inch from the right margin:
    DRAG: right indent marker to the left by 1 inch (to 5 inches on the Ruler)

8. To remove the left indent:
    CLICK: Decrease Indent button (⊞)
    Notice that this button has no effect on the right indent marker.

9. To remove the right indent:
    DRAG: right indent marker back to the right margin (at 6 inches on the Ruler)

10. Move the cursor to anywhere in the last paragraph of the "Ethics-Version 2" document.

11. To indent the last paragraph by 1 inch:
CLICK: Increase Indent button (▣) twice

12. A handy keystroke to remember is (CTRL) + q; it removes all paragraph formatting characteristics from the current paragraph. To demonstrate:
PRESS: (CTRL) + q
The paragraph indentations return to their normal settings against the left and right margins.

13. Move to the end of the document and insert a new blank line.

14. In this next step, you insert a hanging indent where the first line of the paragraph lines up with the left margin and the remainder of the paragraph is indented. To begin:
DRAG: left indent marker to 1 inch on the Ruler
(*Caution*: Make sure that the tip of your mouse pointer points to the triangle and not to the bottom rectangle when dragging. If performed correctly, the first-line indent marker should remain at the margin.)

15. TYPE: Summary
PRESS: (TAB)

16. TYPE: Information systems technology provides a clear opportunity for the disabled to perform in the workplace.
Your screen should now appear similar to Figure 2.11.

FIGURE 2.11

INDENTING
PARAGRAPHS IN THE
"ETHICS-VERSION 2"
DOCUMENT

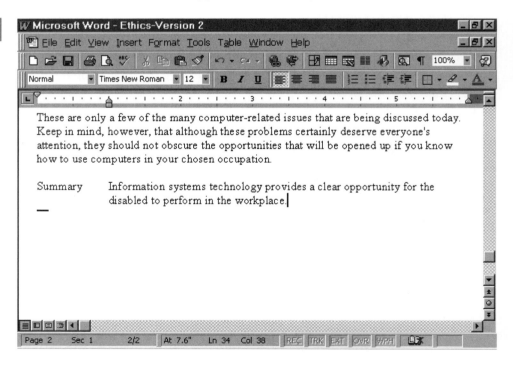

17. Save the "Ethics-Version 2" document to your Data Files location.

18. Close the document.

- **To indent a paragraph from the left margin:**
  CLICK: Increase Indent button ( )
- **To remove a left indent for a paragraph**
  CLICK: Decrease Indent button ( )
- **To customize the first-line, left, and right indents:**
  DRAG: the indent markers on the Ruler

CREATING BULLETED AND NUMBERED LISTS

Word provides a utility for automatically creating lists with leading **bullets** or numbers. Although round circles are the standard shape for bullets, you can select shapes from a variety of symbols. Numbered lists can use numerals, letters, or numbers. If you want to modify the bullet symbols or numbering scheme, choose the Format, Bullets and Numbering command to display the dialog box appearing in Figure 2.12. This screen graphic also shows the resulting dialog box when you click the Customize button.

FIGURE 2.12

BULLETS AND
NUMBERING
DIALOG BOX

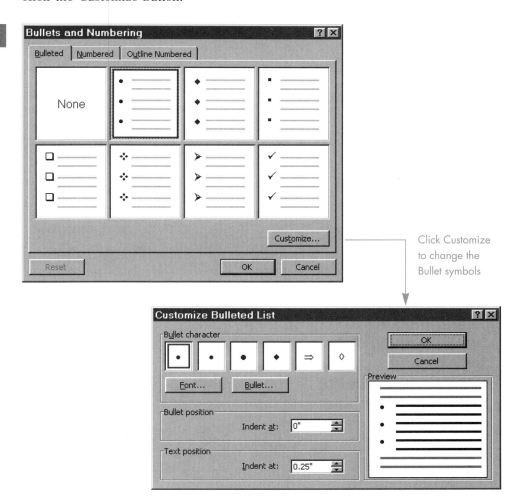

Click Customize
to change the
Bullet symbols

In this section you create bulleted and numbered lists.

Perform the following steps . . .

1. If you do not have an empty document on the screen, open a new document using the New button (□).

2. TYPE: To Do List
PRESS: ENTER twice

3. To create a bulleted list:
CLICK: Bullets button (▤)
A bullet appears and the left indent marker is moved on the Ruler.

4. Enter the following text, pressing ENTER at the end of each line:
Pick up dry cleaning
Meet Jesse at the gym
Go grocery shopping
Mail letter to Mom

5. You will notice that Word automatically starts each new line with a bullet when you press ENTER. To turn off the bullets, ensure that your insertion point is on the line below "Mail letter to Mom" and then:
CLICK: Bullets button (▤)

6. PRESS: ENTER

7. In this next example, you create a numbered list after you've already entered information into your document. To begin:
TYPE: Travel Itinerary
PRESS: ENTER twice

8. Enter the following lines of text, as before:
Aug 12: Flight 455 to Sydney.
Aug 28: Flight 87 to Auckland.
Aug 29: Flight A101 to Christchurch.
Sep 11: Flight 110 to Vancouver.

9. Using the mouse pointer in the Selection bar, select the text that you just entered in step 8.

10. CLICK: Numbering button (▤)
The selected text is automatically numbered.

11. To use letters rather than numbers for the list, position the mouse pointer over the highlighted text and click the right mouse button. From the short-cut menu that appears:
CHOOSE: Bullets and Numbering

12. Ensure that the *Numbered* tab is selected in the dialog box.

13. SELECT: the option that shows a), b), and c)

14. PRESS: ENTER or CLICK: OK
CLICK: anywhere in the document to remove the highlighting
Your document should now appear similar to Figure 2.13.

FIGURE 2.13

NUMBERED AND
BULLETED LISTS

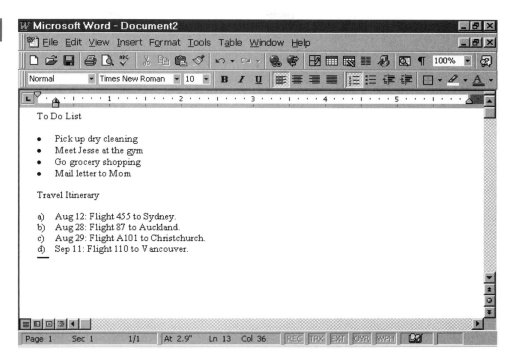

15. To add an item to your travel itinerary between Christchurch and Vancouver, position the I-beam pointer at the end of the Christchurch line or item c) and press **ENTER**.

16. TYPE: `Sep 10: Flight 904 to Seattle.`
Notice that Word automatically renumbers, or in this case re-letters, the list for you when you insert new entries.

17. Save the document as "To Do List" to the Data Files location.

18. Close the document.

QUICK REFERENCE
Bulleted and
Numbered Lists

- **To create a bulleted list, click the Bullets button (▤)**
- **To create a numbered list, click the Numbering button (▤)**
- **To modify the bullet symbols or numbering scheme:**
  CHOOSE: Format, Bullets and Numbering

CHANGING PARAGRAPH ALIGNMENT

Justification refers to how text aligns with the margins of a document. You can align or apply justification to a paragraph either before or after text is typed. Word provides four different types of justification or alignment:

- *Left justification* aligns text at the left margin but leaves jagged right edges as a typewriter does.

- *Center justification* centers the line or paragraph between the margins.

● *Right justification* positions text flush against the right margin.

● *Full justification* provides even text columns at the left and right margins by automatically spacing words on the line.

You specify the justification for a paragraph using the Format, Paragraph command, Formatting toolbar buttons, or keyboard shortcut combinations (summarized in Table 2.5). Remember, paragraph formatting requires the insertion point to be placed in the paragraph to be formatted, but you need not select any text.

TABLE 2.5

Alignment options

Toolbar Button	Keyboard Shortcut	Description
▤	CTRL +1	Left-aligns the selected paragraph
▤	CTRL +e	Centers the selected paragraph
▤	CTRL +r	Right-aligns the selected paragraph
▤	CTRL +j	Fully justifies the selected paragraph

In this section you practice changing justification.

Perform the following steps . . .

1. Retrieve the "Ethics" document from the Advantage Files location.

2. To change the justification for the title, first position the insertion point at the beginning of the title.

3. CLICK: Center button (▤)
   The line is immediately centered between the two margins.

4. CLICK: Align Right button (▤)
   The line is positioned flush against the right margin.

5. To move the line back to its original position:
   CLICK: Align Left button (▤)

6. Practice changing the first paragraph's justification using the buttons on the Formatting toolbar.

QUICK REFERENCE
Changing Alignment

● **To left-align a paragraph, click the Align Left button (▤)**
● **To center a paragraph, click the Center button (▤)**
● **To right-align a paragraph, click the Align Right button (▤)**
● **To fully justify a paragraph, click the Justify button (▤)**

IN ADDITION ALIGNING TEXT VERTICALLY

On a page, text is usually aligned with the top margin. That is, the first line of text that you type prints on the first line after the top margin. In some cases, such as when including a cover page or a table of data in your document, you may want the text to be centered or justified between the top and bottom margins.

To align text vertically, choose File, Page Setup from the Menu bar. Select the *Layout* tab. In the *Vertical alignment* list, select Center to center the text on the page or *Justified* to spread the paragraphs evenly between the top and bottom margins.

CHANGING LINE SPACING

Another common paragraph formatting procedure lets you change the line spacing in a document. The standard options for line spacing are single- and double-spaced, but your choices aren't limited to these. You can specify various line spacing options using the Format, Paragraph dialog box. However, the shortcut keys in Table 2.6 provide the quickest methods for selecting line spacing in a paragraph.

TABLE 2.6	*Keyboard Shortcut*	*Description*
Changing Line Spacing	`CTRL` + 1	Single-spaces the selected paragraph
	`CTRL` + 2	Double-spaces the selected paragraph
	`CTRL` + 5	Applies 1.5-line spaces to the selected paragraph

Now you practice changing line spacing.

Perform the following steps . . .

1. Move the insertion point into the first paragraph of the "Ethics" document.

2. To double-space this paragraph:
   PRESS: `CTRL` + 2
   Notice that only the first paragraph is double-spaced.

3. To apply 1.5-line-spacing:
   PRESS: `CTRL` + 5

4. To return the paragraph to single spacing:
   PRESS: `CTRL` + 1

5. To double-space the document, you need to first select the entire document. Move the mouse pointer into the Selection bar and triple-click the left mouse button. The entire document should be highlighted in reverse video before proceeding.

6. PRESS: `CTRL` + 2
   The "Ethics" document should be double-spaced.

7. CLICK: anywhere in the document to remove the highlighting

8. Close the document and do not save the changes.

QUICK REFERENCE
Line Spacing Shortcuts

- To single-space a paragraph, select the text, then press CTRL +1
- To space a paragraph by 1.5 lines, then press CTRL +5
- To double-space a paragraph, then press CTRL +2
- To select a specific line spacing option:
  CHOOSE: Format, Paragraph
  CLICK: down arrow beside the *Line Spacing* drop-down list box
  SELECT: the desired spacing
  PRESS: ENTER or CLICK: OK

CHANGING TAB SETTINGS

Tabs enable you to neatly enter text and numbers into columns. If your past experience includes using a typewriter, you are likely familiar with using the Space Bar to line up columns of text on a page. This works fine when you are using a monospaced font in which all letters are an equal width. However, most word processing fonts are not monospaced and, therefore, you cannot line up columns by simply pressing the Space Bar a fixed number of times. To accomplish the same objective in Word, you place tabs on the Ruler and use the TAB key to move the insertion point between tab stops. The four basic types of tabs are described in Table 2.7 below.

TABLE 2.7

Types of Tabs

Tab Name	Ruler Symbol	Description
Left-Aligned	L	Starting at the tab, text extends to the right as you type
Center-Aligned	⊥	Starting at the tab, text is centered on the tab stop.
Right-Aligned	⌐	Starting at the tab, text extends to the left as you type.
Decimal-Aligned	⊥	At the tab, the integer portion of a number extends to the left and the decimal fraction extends to the right.

Before you start adding your own tabs to the Ruler, you should be aware that Word supplies left-aligned tabs every 0.5 inch by default. If you require greater flexibility, you begin by selecting a tab type using the Tab Alignment button (L) located at the far left of the Ruler. On each mouse click, Word switches to the next tab symbol. Once the desired tab type appears, you position the tip of the mouse pointer on the Ruler and click once to place the tab. If you need to fine-tune a tab's position on the Ruler, you simply drag it back and forth. To remove a tab, you drag it downwards and off the Ruler. Be forewarned that all the default tabs to the left of the new tab are automatically cleared.

You can also set tabs using the Format, Tabs command (its dialog box appears in Figure 2.14.) An added benefit to using the Tabs dialog box to set tabs is that you can also set leaders. A tab **leader** is a dotted, dashed, or solid line that fills the space between text and tab stops. Leaders are commonly used in tables of contents to visually join the section headings with the page numbers. Some examples of leaders are provided below:

Dot leader ....A Right-Aligned tab
Dashed leader --------------------------Another Right-Aligned tab
Solid leader _____And yet a third Right-Aligned tab

FIGURE 2.14

TABS DIALOG BOX

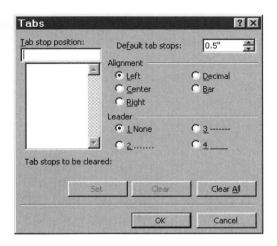

Next you create a document that uses customized tabs.

Perform the following steps . . .

1. If you do not have an empty document on the screen, open a new document using the New button (□).

2. To center the title and specify double spacing:
   CLICK: Center button (▤)
   PRESS: CTRL +2

3. TYPE: Marketing Memo
   PRESS: ENTER

4. To change the paragraph alignment to fully justified:
   CLICK: Justify button (▤)

5. TYPE: It is my pleasure to announce to Sporting Life's marketing and sales staff that sales have increased steadily for the past six months. As you well know, Sporting Life is known for carrying quality sporting items at reasonable prices. But without you, Sporting Life would be "just another sports store." Keep up the good work!

6. To add a blank line and change to single spacing:
PRESS: (**ENTER**)
PRESS: (**CTRL**)+1

In the remainder of the document, you will create an income and expense report for January through June. The first step is to label the columns that will contain the figures. The first column heading will be centered at 3 inches and the second column heading at 4.5 inches on the Ruler.

Now you set tab stops for the table heading and the data.

Perform the following steps . . .

1. CLICK: Tab Alignment button at the far left of the Ruler until the center-aligned tab symbol (⊥) appears

2. Position the tip of the mouse pointer on the 3-inch mark of the Ruler and click the left mouse button once. If done properly, you will see a center-aligned tab mark appear on the Ruler. If the tab stop is not placed correctly, drag the tab mark into position using the mouse. If you need to, you can delete the tab and start over by dragging the tab downward and off the Ruler.

3. To position the second tab stop, position the mouse pointer on the 4.5-inch mark and click the left mouse button once.

4. PRESS: (**TAB**)
The insertion point moves to the first tab stop. Notice that Word deletes the default tab stops to the left of the customized tabs.

5. TYPE: REVENUE
PRESS: (**TAB**)

6. TYPE: EXPENSES
PRESS: (**ENTER**) twice
The headings are centered on their respective tab marks.

7. The next step is to set the decimal tabs for aligning the numbers correctly. Before proceeding, remove the two center-aligned tab stops by dragging them down and off the Ruler.

8. To specify a tab position for the row headings:
SELECT: Left-aligned tab (L) using the Tab Alignment button
CLICK: 1 inch on the Ruler

9. To specify a tab position for the REVENUE figures:
SELECT: Decimal-aligned tab (⊥) using the Tab Alignment button
CLICK: 3.25 inches on the Ruler
(*Tip:* To display a measurement helper, try holding down the (**ALT**) key as you drag the tab symbol on the Ruler.)

10. To specify a tab position for the EXPENSES figures:
CLICK: 4.75 inches on the Ruler

11. For fun, let's turn on the Show/Hide symbols feature:
CLICK: Show/Hide button (¶)

12. Now, let's enter January's REVENUE and EXPENSES:
PRESS: `TAB`
TYPE: January
PRESS: `TAB`
TYPE: 18,900.75
PRESS: `TAB`
TYPE: 13,534.67
PRESS: `ENTER`
Notice that each press of the `TAB` key results in the tab symbol (→).

13. Enter the following information in the Month, Revenue, and Expense columns to finish the Marketing Memo:

February	22,050.00	15,356.48
March	17,354.45	11,225.32
April	18,239.00	15,006.95
May	26,884.69	19,322.55
June	28,677.41	21,632.10

14. Save the document as "Marketing Memo" to the Data Files location. Your screen should now appear similar to Figure 2.15.

15. Print the "Marketing Memo" document.

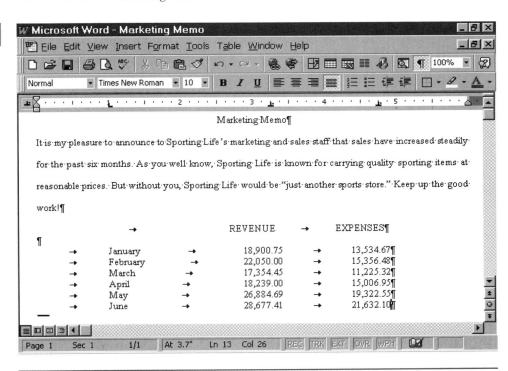

1. **SELECT: a tab type (⌊, ⊥, ⌋, or ⊥) using the Tab Alignment button on the Ruler**

2. **CLICK: desired location on the Ruler to set the tab stop**

FORCING A PAGE BREAK

Word automatically repaginates a document as you insert and delete text. In Word's Normal view, a dotted line appears wherever Word inserts a floating page break, sometimes splitting an important paragraph or a table of figures. Rather than leaving the text on separate pages, you can instruct Word to start a new page at the insertion point by inserting a hard page break. The quickest way to force a hard page break is to press CTRL + ENTER. You can also choose the Insert, Break command from the Menu bar.

In this section, you force a page break so that the table created in the "Marketing Memo" document appears on a separate page.

Perform the following steps . . .

1. Position the insertion point at the beginning of the line containing the headings REVENUE and EXPENSES. Make sure that the insertion point is in the first column, next to the left margin.

2. PRESS: CTRL + ENTER
A solid line with the words "Page Break" appears above the headings. The Status bar should now contain "Page 2" and "2/2."

3. To delete the hard page break, position the insertion point directly on the page break line and press DELETE.

4. Close the "Marketing Memo" document without saving.

QUICK REFERENCE
Inserting a Forced Page Break

1. **Position the insertion point at the beginning of the line that you want moved to the top of a new page.**
2. **PRESS: CTRL + ENTER**

AUTOCORRECT FEATURES

Word is pretty eager to please. In fact, Word can perform a number of formatting tasks for you automatically. Depending on your preference, Word will format your documents as you type or once you're finished. You specify what you want Word to do for you by choosing Tools, AutoCorrect from the Menu bar.

By default, Word formats your documents automatically as you type. Word can format your documents with borders, numbered and bulleted lists, quotations, em dashes, ordinal numbers such as 1st, fractions such as ¼, and symbols such as © and ™. It can even help you complete certain words, such as the months of the year, the names of Fortune 1000 companies, and cities with a population greater than 30,000. In this section, you create a small document that illustrates some of these features.

Perform the following steps . . .

1. To begin a new document:
   CLICK: New button (▢) on the Standard toolbar

2. While you work through this section, we assume the *AutoCorrect* and *Auto-Format As You Type* tabs on your computer look the same as those in Figure 2.16. To check these settings:
   CHOOSE: Tools, AutoCorrect from the Menu bar
   CLICK: *AutoCorrect* tab
   Ensure that the settings match those in Figure 2.16.
   CLICK: *AutoFormat As You Type* tab
   Again, ensure that the settings match those in Figure 2.16.

FIGURE 2.16

AUTOCORRECT DIALOG BOX: CHECKING YOUR SETTINGS

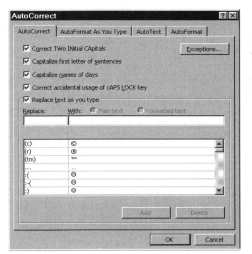
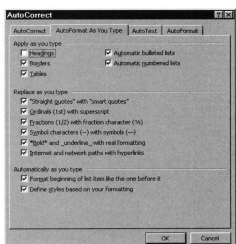

3. When you are finished:
   PRESS: **ENTER** or CLICK: OK button

4. Let's begin by typing a heading for our document.
   TYPE: **AutoFormat As You Type**
   PRESS: **ENTER**
   Word thinks "As" should be "as" and has thus underlined "As" with a wavy green underline. Ignore this suggestion.

5. To apply a border using the AutoFormat feature:
   TYPE: ---
   PRESS: **ENTER**
   A border now appears beneath the title.

6. To insert a blank line after the border:
   PRESS: **ENTER**

7. To automatically create a numbered list, you type the first number, press (TAB), type some text, and then press (ENTER). To illustrate:
TYPE: 1.
PRESS: (TAB) once
TYPE: Apples
PRESS: (ENTER)
TYPE: Oranges
PRESS: (ENTER)
TYPE: Bananas

8. To stop the automatic numbering:
PRESS: (ENTER) twice

9. To automatically create a bulleted list, you type an asterisk (*), press (TAB), type some text, and then press (ENTER). To illustrate:
TYPE: *
PRESS: (TAB) once
TYPE: Cookies
PRESS: (ENTER)
TYPE: Ice Cream
PRESS: (ENTER)
TYPE: Cake

10. To stop the automatic bullets:
PRESS: (ENTER) twice

11. In this step, you'll see how Word automatically formats ordinal numbers, fractions, and other symbols. Just type the characters you see; Word will do the formatting for you.
To type an ordinal number:
TYPE: 1
TYPE: s
TYPE: t
TYPE: , (comma)
PRESS: Space Bar

On the same line, type the following literals to display the associated symbols. Type a comma and then press the Space Bar after each symbol appears.

You Type:	To display:
1/4	¼
(c)	©
(r)	®
(tm)	™
-->	→
==>	➜
:)	☺
:|	☺
:(	☹

12. To insert a blank line:
PRESS: [ENTER]

13. Using the mouse pointer in the Selection bar, select the row of symbols you entered in step 11. Then:
SELECT: 14-point size from the *Font Size* drop-down list ([10 ▼])
CLICK: anywhere in the document to remove the highlight
Your screen should now appear similar to Figure 2.17.

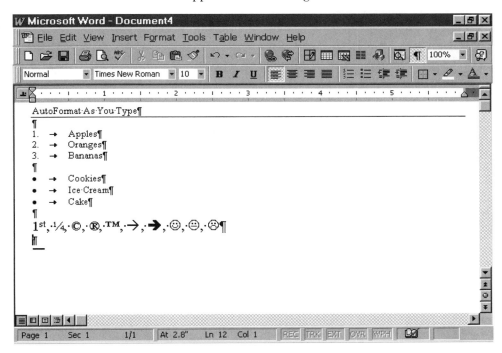

14. Word 97 includes a feature called AutoText, which automatically finishes commonly used words such as "January," "Respectfully," and "CONFIDEN-TIAL." You simply type a few characters and Word will help you type the rest. Before illustrating the use of this feature, move the cursor to the end of the document.
PRESS: [CTRL] + [END]
PRESS: [ENTER] twice

15. TYPE: `I leave for vacation in Janu`
Your screen should now appear similar to Figure 2.18.

FIGURE 2.18

ILLUSTRATING THE
AUTOCOMPLETE FEATURE

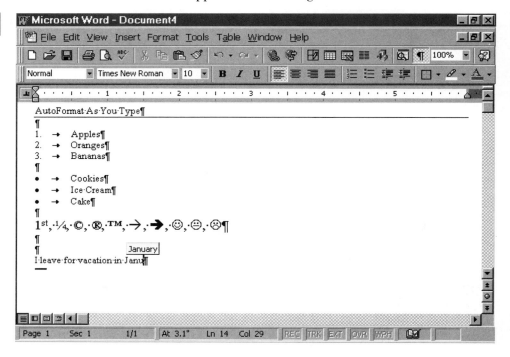

16. To let Word complete the Word for you, you press (ENTER).
PRESS: (ENTER)
"January" should now appear. Type a period (.) to end the sentence.

17. To see the complete list of words that Word will help you type:
CHOOSE: Tools, AutoCorrect
CLICK: *AutoText* tab

18. Scroll through the list of words and phrases in the *Enter AutoText entries here* list box. In a later session, we show you how to create your own Auto-Text entries.

19. To return to your document:
CLICK: Cancel button

20. Save the document as "AutoFormat" to your Data Files location.

21. Close the document.

IN ADDITION AUTOMATIC HYPERLINK FORMATTING

By default, Word will format any Internet, network, and e-mail addresses that you include in your documents as hyperlinks. You then simply click the hyperlink to go to the specified location. Word automatically underlines and applies a blue attribute to your hyperlinks. For example, the following shows a hyperlink to Microsoft Word on the web: http://www.microsoft.com/word/

SUMMARY

This session introduced several methods for moving around a document and selecting text. As with most Windows programs, Word is based upon a Select and then Do approach to formatting and editing. Therefore, the proper selection of text is extremely important for executing commands and working effectively with Word.

This session concentrated on character and paragraph formatting commands. Besides applying boldface, italic, and underline character styles to text, character formatting involves changing the typeface, font, and point size. Paragraph formatting commands enable you to customize paragraphs in your text without affecting the entire document. This section explored indenting paragraphs, creating bulleted and numbered lists, aligning text, setting tabs, and forcing page breaks. You then practiced using some of Word's AutoFormat features.

Table 2.8 provides a summary of the commands introduced in this session.

TABLE 2.8

Command Summary

Task Description	Menu Command	Toolbar Button	Keyboard Shortcut
Move to a specific location in your document	Edit, Go To		CTRL+g, or F5
Make text bold	Format, Font	B	CTRL+b
Italicize text		I	CTRL+i
Underline text		U	CTRL+u
Highlight text		🖍▾	
Color text		A▾	
Animate text	Format, Font, Animation tab		
Select a typeface	Format, Font	Times New Roman ▾	
Change the font size		10 ▾	
Increase Indent	Format,	⬛	
Decrease Indent	Paragraph	⬛	
Create a bulleted list	Format, Bullets	☰	
Create a numbered list	and Numbering	☰	
Specify bullet symbols or numbering schemes	Format, Bullets and Numbering		
Provide options for setting up your page layout	File, Page Setup		

TABLE 2.8
Continued

Task Description	Menu Command	Toolbar Button	Keyboard Shortcut
Left-align a paragraph	Format,	≣	CTRL +1
Center-align a paragraph	Paragraph	≣	CTRL +e
Right-align a paragraph		≣	CTRL +r
Justify a paragraph		≣	CTRL +j
Single-space a paragraph	Format,		CTRL +1
Space a paragraph by 1.5 lines	Paragraph		CTRL +5
Double-space a paragraph			CTRL +2
Specifies tab positions and leaders	Format, Tabs		
Copy formatting options		◇	
Force a page break	Insert, Break		CTRL + ENTER

K EY TERMS

bullets

The symbols used to set apart points in a document. Bullets are typically round dots and appear in paragraphs with a hanging indent.

default settings

Assumptions made by Word, if no other specific selections are made.

font

All of the symbols and characters of a particular typeface for a given point size.

leader

The symbols, lines, dots, or dashes that fill the gap between text and tab stops.

Paragraph Symbol

The symbol (¶) at the end of a paragraph that stores all of Word's paragraph formatting information.

Selection bar

The leftmost column of the document window. The Selection bar provides shortcut methods for selecting text in a document using the mouse.

typeface

A style of print.

EXERCISES

SHORT ANSWER

1. How do you select an entire document using the mouse?

2. What are Word's default settings?

3. What procedure would you use to move efficiently to page 2, line 16?

4. How would you go about selecting a single sentence?

5. Describe the four types of tabs you can include in a document.

6. Describe some methods for moving the cursor around a document.

7. Provide an example of when you would use a dot leader.

8. How would you set line spacing to 1.5 lines?

9. Describe the most efficient procedure for selecting and then adding animation to a paragraph.

10. What is the difference between a hard page break and a floating page break? How can you tell the difference between the two in a Word document?

HANDS-ON

(*Note:* Ensure that you know the location of your Advantage Files and where to store your Data Files. If necessary, ask your instructor or lab assistant for additional information.)

1. Create the memo appearing in Figure 2.19. Make sure to include the current date in the DATE: area and your name in the FROM: area of the memo.

FIGURE 2.19

"KATHY JORDAN"
DOCUMENT

MEMORANDUM

DATE: *current date*

  TO: Kathy Jordan
           Administrative Support Manager

FROM: *your name*
           V.P., Marketing

 SUBJECT: Appearance of Documents

It has come to my attention that our two clients are finding our proposals difficult to read. When queried further, they both mentioned (as personal preference dictates) that the sentences seemed to have gaps between the words. (Similar to this paragraph.)

After speaking with several people in our Word Processing department, I understand that we have been using full justification for paragraphs. As these two clients are our lifeblood, please prepare a letter to the staff stating that the use of full justification in documents is no longer acceptable. All documents are to be typed using left justification only.

Please send me a draft of the letter by Monday.

Enjoy your weekend!

a. Make sure that your memo has the following formatting features:
    - Center the title "MEMORANDUM."
    - Use tabs to right-align the memo headings for DATE:, TO:, FROM:, and SUBJECT:.
    - Fully justify the first paragraph.
    - Left-align (or left-justify) the second and third paragraphs.
    - Right-align (or right-justify) the last line.

b. Make the title and the memo headings (DATE:, TO:, FROM:, and SUBJECT:) bold.

c. Italicize the word "justification" throughout the memo.

    d. Underline "Monday" in the third paragraph.

    e. Save the document as "Kathy Jordan" to your Data Files location.

    f. Print the document.

    g. Close the document.

2. This exercise uses tabs to align a table of numbers.

    a. Open a new document.

    b. Specify decimal tab settings on the Ruler at 2 inches, 3.5 inches, and 5 inches.

    c. Enter the following information into the document.

	January	February	March
East	50,000	65,000	75,000
West	125,000	105,000	100,500
Central	55,000	50,000	75,000

    d. PRESS: (ENTER) three times.

    e. TYPE: These are the forecasted commissions for the first part of 1997. Please add a discussion of these figures to the Sales Planning agenda next week.

    f. Save the document as "Forecast" to your Data Files location.

    g. Print the document.

    h. Close the document.

3. The objective of this exercise is to practice using tabs, leaders, and character formatting commands.

    a. Open a new document.

    b. Create the document appearing in Figure 2.20.

FIGURE 2.20

"SALES PLANNING
AGENDA" DOCUMENT

SALES PLANNING AGENDA

DATE: October 4th, 1997   TIME: 9 A.M. to 4 P.M.

Who Is Our Customer?
    Demographic Analysis . . . . . . 9:00-9:45 A.M.
    Psychographic Analysis . . . . . 9:50-10:30 A.M.
    Lifestyles and AIO Study . . 10:45 A.M.-12 P.M.

What Are We Selling?
    Research and Development . . . . 1:00-2:00 P.M.
    Product Packaging . . . . 2:05-2:45 P.M.
    Pricing Structures . . . . 3:00-3:30 P.M.

Incentives and Commissions . . . . . 3:35-4:00 P.M.

Please be prepared to give a ten-minute impromptu
presentation on the status of your department.
Specifically, mention the following issues:

- Employee Productivity
- Employee Satisfaction
- Resource Management
- Future Requirements

                    Your faithful V.P. of Marketing,

                                        your name

c.   Make the first two lines of the agenda, including the title, date, and time, bold.

d.   Increase the font size for the title to 18 points.

e.   Select the Arial font for the main agenda items. (*Note:* If Arial isn't present on your computer, select a different font.)

f.   Make the three main agenda items bold and 14 points in size.

g.   Underline the word "faithful" in the closing of the document.

h.   Save the document as "Sales Planning Agenda" to your Data Files location.

i.   Print the agenda.

j.   Close the document.

4.   The objective of this exercise is to practice including a page break in a document, changing the font of an entire document, indenting, and changing line spacing.

a. Create the document pictured in Figure 2.21 (make sure to perform the steps described in brackets):

FIGURE 2.21

"POINTING DEVICES"
DOCUMENT

THE POPULAR POINTING DEVICES
USED WITH MICROCOMPUTERS

DATE: *current date*
BY: *your name*

[*insert a page break here*]

The following is a summary of the types of pointing
     devices that are commonly used with
     microcomputers:

The mouse: A small, hand-held device connected to
     the computer by a cable and rolled around the
     desktop to move the cursor around the screen.

The trackball: Essentially an upside down mouse.
     The ball is rolled around in a socket to move
     the cursor. Trackballs are used where space is
     limited.

The light pen: A pen-shaped input device that uses
     a photoelectric (light-sensitive) cell to
     signal screen position to the computer. The
     pen, which is connected to the computer by a
     cable, is placed on the display screen at the
     desired location.

The touch screen: A special display screen that is
     sensitive to touch. The user touches the screen
     at desired locations, marked by labeled boxes,
     to "point out" choices to the computer.

The digitizer: A tablet covered by a grid of wires
     that are connected to the computer by a cable.
     Drawings placed on the tablet can be traced
     with a special pen or mouse-like device to
     translate the image into computer-usable code.

Pen-based computing: Uses special software and
     hardware to interpret handwriting done directly
     on the screen.

b. Before you continue, save the document to your Data Files location as "Pointing Devices."

c. Double-space the entire document.

d. Change the font of the entire document to Arial.

e. Increase the point size of the title on the first page to 16 point.

f. Center all the text positioned on the first page.

g. Boldface the name of each pointing device on page 2.

h. Save the document as "Pointing Devices" to your Data Files location.

i. Print the document.

j. Close the document.

5. On your own, create a resume that includes your name and address centered at the top of the page. (*Note*: Except for your name, it is acceptable to use fictitious information in the resume.) Include character and paragraph formatting to emphasize important events. Make sure to review the page setup settings (margins, etc.) and edit them if you think your resume will look better. Save the resume as "On Your Own-3" to your Data Files location and then print the resume. *Extra Credit*: Align the resume so that it is centered vertically on the page.

6. On your own, create an itinerary. Your destination is a city you have never been to but would like to visit. For each day in this weeklong vacation, detail the types of activities, such as taking a tour or visiting a monument, that you will be doing. Be sure to use character, paragraph, and page formatting commands when creating the itinerary in order to describe your vacation in an organized fashion. Save the itinerary as "On Your Own-4" to your Data Files location and then print the itinerary.

CASE PROBLEMS   **ADVANCED SOFTWARE DESIGN, INC.**

(*Note:* In the following case problems, assume the role of the primary characters and perform the same steps that they identify. You may want to re-read the session opening.)

1. For the past year, Mary's proposals have all looked similar to the one appearing in Figure 2.22. She wants to create a new document that contains the same information but with formatting enhancements. For example, she would like to make the company's name and address look more like a letterhead on printed stationery, perhaps centered and with a different font at the top of the page. She would also like to add emphasis to the different titles on the proposal (Date, Client Name, Project Description, and so on).

    Create the document appearing in Figure 2.22 and then perform the steps that Mary has identified. Print it and then save the document as "ASD Proposal" to your Data Files location. Lastly, close the document before proceeding.

FIGURE 2.22

A STANDARD ASD
PROPOSAL DOCUMENT

```
ADVANCED SOFTWARE DESIGN, INC.
221 FOREST DRIVE
Lakewood, NJ 08701
Tel: 333-333-3333
Fax: 333-333-3331

DATE: [enter current date]

CLIENT NAME: [enter client name]

PROJECT DESCRIPTION: [enter project description]

HOUR ESTIMATE: [enter hours]

COST ESTIMATE: [multiply the hours by $50]



Signature _____
              Alethia Montera, Vice President
```

2. Having just completed a telephone conversation with Mountain Wear, Inc., Alethia hands Mary her proposal notes for typing. The project description reads as follows:

   Mountain Wear, Inc., a manufacturer of rugged footwear, needs a better program for keeping track of its inventory. It has one warehouse, with several truckloads of shoes coming and going each day. The company would like to generate hourly reports and gather demographic data on the people who buy Mountain Wear shoes. I estimate this job will take 122 programming hours.

   Mary retrieves the "ASD Proposal" document from the Data Files location and edits it to include the information from Alethia's notes. When finished, she prints it and then saves the proposal as "MWI Proposal" to the Data Files location. Lastly, Mary closes the document.

3. Now that Alethia has seen what Mary can do with Microsoft Word, she asks Mary to format the company's client list for the upcoming board meeting. She gives Mary the following instructions:

   Mary, you will find the document file, called "Clients," at the Advantage Files location. Please format the contents to make it look more professional. Thanks, Alethia.

Upon retrieving the "Clients" document, Mary decides to print it so that she can get a complete picture of the document before she applies any formatting commands. With the printed document in hand, Mary sees clearly that she needs to center and apply a larger point size to the title. Also, she decides to indent and number the names, format all text using the Times New Roman font, and add emphasis to the company names by making them italic. After incorporating her changes, she saves the file to the Data Files location as "Clients-Formatted."

Mary now decides to preview the "Clients-Formatted" document on the screen to see if she likes the overall look of the document. Although pleased with the list, she decides to insert some extra blank lines at the top of the document and a few just below the main heading to balance the page. Mary saves the document again, prints it, and puts a copy in the message box outside Alethia's office.

4. Upon returning to her cubicle, Mary finds a note tacked to her computer monitor from Alethia.

Mary, I need someone to create a splashy advertising piece for an upcoming customer mailing, and I think you're the one to do it! Use one side of an 8x10 piece of paper. I want you to make the following points: (1) Advanced Software Design can satisfy any programming requirement because of its staff of highly talented programmers. (2) ASD always supplies accurate cost estimates. (3) Your satisfaction is guaranteed—should you be dissatisfied with a product, we'll either modify it at our own cost or give you a full refund. (4) ASD provides a 24-hour support hotline should questions arise once an application is delivered. And lastly, after the name, address, and phone number of our company (positioned at the top of the page), try to draw the reader's attention to the following sentence: The Small Business Association, in conjunction with the Hapstead Publishing Group, did an assessment of software development companies and gave Advanced Software Design the "Best Pick" award for 1996. By the way, I need this by tomorrow. Let me know if you have any questions. Thanks, Alethia.

Although she's flattered, it's already late in the day and Mary is concerned about completing the advertising piece on time. She realizes that without Microsoft Word she won't stand a chance at finishing this ad. When you finish the project, print the document and then save it as "ASD Advertisement" to the Data Files location. Lastly, close the document and Exit Word.

Microsoft Word 97 for Windows

Editing and Proofing Tools

SESSION

3

HTTP WWW

IRWIN
COMPUTER & INFORMATION TECHNOLOGY

SESSION OUTLINE

INTRODUCTION

By the completion of this session, you will know the editing commands required to develop error-free documents. Also, you'll learn how to use Word's proofing tools including the Spelling and Grammar Checker and the Thesaurus. Whether you require assistance with spelling, sentence structure, or just finding the right word, these tools are invaluable.

THE *RIVER REPORT*

The *River Report* is a weekly publication that provides news reports, announcements, and general interest stories for the Sacramento River region. Linda James, a graduate of Stanford's journalism program, has just accepted the position of editor for the small-town newspaper. In her new position, Linda is responsible for identifying leads, editing articles written by her reporters, and, most importantly, getting the paper out every Friday.

Her new office is well-appointed with a large oak desk and a new Pentium™ computer system. On the computer screen, her predecessor, Hank Leary, left the following message:

Linda, welcome! Just so you know, the reporters will be submitting their articles on disk for you to edit and print using Microsoft Word. They should have their articles in to you each week by 7:00 P.M. on Wednesday. You have all day Thursday to edit and proof their work. The articles must be sent to Production by 7:00 P.M. on Thursday to meet the deadline. Hope all goes well. Hank.

Linda feels a swelling anxiety overcome her. It's already Wednesday afternoon and, although she has used Microsoft Word before, she has never performed the types of editing tasks that will be required of her to edit and proof these articles. She only has a few short hours to become skilled at editing articles using her fancy new computer!

In this session, you and Linda will learn how to copy and move text within a document, search for and replace text, and use Word's proofing tools.

WORKING WITH MULTIPLE DOCUMENTS

Word allows you to simultaneously display and work with as many documents as your computer's memory will allow. This feature enables you to open multiple documents at the same time and share information among them. You can also use the Window, New Window command to open multiple windows or views of the same document. For example, you might want to view page 10 of a document while working on page 30. Each document or window view appears in its own document window. These windows can be sized, moved, and arranged anywhere in the document area.

In this section you display multiple documents.

Perform the following steps . . .

1. Make sure that you've loaded Microsoft Word and that you've identified the location for retrieving your Advantage Files and the location for storing your Data Files. If you require a diskette, place it into the diskette drive now.

2. To close all open documents that may appear in the document area:
PRESS: (SHIFT) and hold it down
CHOOSE: File, Close All
(*Note:* By holding down the (SHIFT) key, Word changes the command in the pull-down menu from Close to Close All.)

3. Retrieve the "Spelling" document from the Advantage Files location.

4. Retrieve the "Sailboat" document from the Advantage Files location.

5. When the "Sailboat" document is opened, the "Spelling" document disappears. Actually, the "Sailboat" document is just temporarily covering the "Spelling" document. To display the "Spelling" document:
CHOOSE: Window, 2 Spelling

6. Notice that the names of the open documents appear at the bottom of the Window pull-down menu. To move between open documents, you simply select the document name. To move back to "Sailboat":
CHOOSE: Window, 1 Sailboat

7. Although this method allows you to work on several documents at the same time, sometimes it's desirable to compare documents side-by-side. To simultaneously display both documents:
CHOOSE: Window, Arrange All
Your screen should now appear similar to Figure 3.1.

FIGURE 3.1

USING THE WINDOW, ARRANGE ALL COMMAND TO VIEW TWO DOCUMENTS

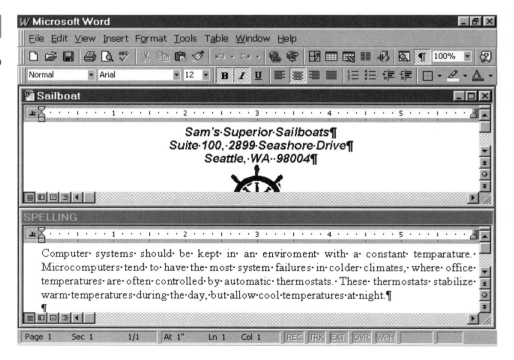

8. The document window with the icon (Sailboat) is the active window. Any editing and formatting commands that you execute will affect the active window only. To move between documents, you click the mouse pointer on a window to make it active:
CLICK: anywhere in the "Spelling" document window
The "Spelling" Title bar should change color to reflect that it is active and the 🔲 icon will appear at the left side of the Title bar.

9. CLICK: anywhere in the "Sailboat" document window
The "Sailboat" Title bar changes to reflect that it is now active.

10. Notice that the active window has its own Minimize (🔲), Maximize (🔲), and Close buttons (❎). To maximize the "Sailboat" window:
CLICK: Maximize icon (🔲) on the "Sailboat" document window

11. CHOOSE: Window, Arrange All to view both windows again

12. PRESS: (SHIFT) and hold it down
CHOOSE: File, Close All
Both documents are closed and removed from the document area.

QUICK REFERENCE
Viewing Multiple Documents

- **CHOOSE: Window, filename to display an open document**
- **CHOOSE: Window, Arrange All to show multiple windows on-screen**
- **CHOOSE: Window, New Window to open a new document window**

IN ADDITION LINKING YOUR DOCUMENT TO THE INTERNET
AND OTHER MICROSOFT OFFICE DOCUMENTS

You can create links in your document to Internet addresses or to other Microsoft Office documents on your hard drive or network drive. When you click the link, you move to the desired location. These links are called *hyperlinks*. To include hyperlinks in your document, you click the Insert Hyperlink button (🔳) on the Standard

toolbar and then answer the questions in the Insert Hyperlink dialog box.

For more information, choose Help, Contents and Index. Click the *Contents* tab and select the "Working with Online and Internet Documents" topic. Then explore the "Working with Hyperlinks" topic.

COPYING AND MOVING INFORMATION

There are several different methods for copying and moving text in a document. Similar to most Windows applications, Word provides the **Clipboard** for sharing information within a document, among documents, and among applications. For quick "from-here-to-there" copy and move operations, Word provides the **drag and drop** method where you use the mouse to drag text and graphics in a document. This section provides examples using both methods for copying and moving information.

USING THE CLIPBOARD

If the drag and drop method is quicker and easier, why use the Clipboard to copy and move information? The Clipboard provides greater flexibility, allows you to copy information to multiple locations in a document, and allows you to copy and move information to and from other applications. The general process for copying and moving information using the Clipboard is summarized in the following steps:

a. Select the text that you want to copy or move.

b. Cut or copy the selection to the Clipboard.

c. Move the insertion point to where you want to place the information.

d. Paste the information from the Clipboard into the document.

e. Repeat steps c. and d., as desired.

The Clipboard tools for cutting, copying, and pasting text and graphics appear in Table 3.1.

TABLE 3.1 Copying and Moving Information Using the Clipboard	*Task Description*	*Menu Command*	*Toolbar Button*	*Keyboard Shortcut*
	Moves the selected text from the document to the Clipboard	Edit, Cut	✂	CTRL +X
	Copies the selected text to the Clipboard	Edit, Copy	📋	CTRL +C
	Inserts the contents of the Clipboard at the insertion point	Edit, Paste	📋	CTRL +V

In this section you practice using the Clipboard.

Perform the following steps . . .

1. Retrieve the "Hardware" document from the Advantage Files location.

2. If the document window isn't maximized, click its Maximize button (⬜).

3. Insert two lines at the top of the document using the ENTER key.

4. To copy the phrase "Computer systems" from the first sentence to the top of the document, first you must select the text:
   SELECT: Computer systems

5. To copy the selection to the Clipboard:
   CLICK: Copy button (📋)

6. PRESS: ⬆ twice

7. To paste the contents of the Clipboard into the document:
   CLICK: Paste button (📋)

8. To center the title:
   CLICK: Center button (≡)

9. To change the case of the letters in the title:
SELECT: Computer systems
PRESS: (SHIFT) + (F3) once
The title should now read "COMPUTER SYSTEMS." (*Note*: You can also choose the Format, Change Case command.)

10. Let's move the entire second paragraph to the end of the document:
DOUBLE-CLICK: beside the second paragraph in the Selection bar

11. To move the selected paragraph to the Clipboard:
CLICK: Cut button (✂)
Notice that the paragraph is removed from the document.

12. Move to the bottom of the document and add a blank line:
PRESS: (CTRL) + (END)
PRESS: (ENTER)

13. CLICK: Paste button (📋)
The paragraph is inserted at the bottom of the document.

14. Insert another blank line at the end of the document:
PRESS: (ENTER)

15. When information is placed on the Clipboard, it can be pasted multiple times. To illustrate, you will insert another copy of the paragraph:
CLICK: Paste button (📋)
A second copy of the paragraph appears.

QUICK REFERENCE
Copying and Moving
Information Using the
Clipboard

- **To move information using the Clipboard:**
  CLICK: Cut button (✂)
- **To copy information using the Clipboard:**
  CLICK: Copy button (📋)
- **To paste information using the Clipboard:**
  CLICK: Paste button (📋)

IN ADDITION COPYING AND MOVING BETWEEN MICROSOFT OFFICE APPLICATIONS

1. Select the text, data, or other object that you want to move or copy. Then click the Cut button (✂) or the Copy button (📋).

2. Switch to the application you want to move or copy into and then position the cursor.

3. Click the Paste button (📋) to insert the contents of the Clipboard at the cursor location. (*Note*: If you choose Edit, Paste Special from the Menu bar and then choose the Paste Link option, the pasted information will be linked to its source application. Any changes you make to the data in the source application will show up in the linked application.)

IN ADDITION INSERTING AN EXCEL WORKSHEET IN A WORD DOCUMENT

1. Open both the Word document and the Excel workbook.

2. In the Excel workbook:

   a. Select the worksheet or range of cells that you want to copy to Word.

   b. CLICK: Copy button (📋)

3. In the Word document:

   a. Position the cursor where you want to insert the worksheet.

   b. CHOOSE: Edit, Paste Special

   c. Choose Paste (to embed) or Paste link (to link).

IN ADDITION INSERTING AN ENTIRE POWERPOINT PRESENTATION IN A WORD DOCUMENT

1. Open the presentation in PowerPoint for which you want to create a Word document.

2. CHOOSE: File, Send To

3. CHOOSE: Microsoft Word

4. In the Write-Up dialog box, choose how the slides should appear in Word.

5. Choose Paste (to embed) or Paste link (to link).

USING DRAG AND DROP

The drag and drop method is the easiest way to copy and move information short distances. The Clipboard is not used during a drag and drop operation; therefore, you can only copy or move text from one location to another. In other words, you are not able to perform multiple "pastes" of the selected text. This method is extremely quick for simple copy and move operations.

Next you practice using drag and drop.

Perform the following steps . . .

1. In the "Hardware" document, select the first sentence of the first paragraph by positioning the I-beam mouse pointer over any word in the sentence, holding down the **CTRL** key, and clicking once.

2. Position the mouse pointer over the selected text. Notice that the pointer shape is a left-pointing diagonal arrow and not an I-beam. To move this sentence using drag and drop:
   CLICK: left mouse button and hold it down

3. The mouse pointer changes shape to include a phantom insertion point at the end of the diagonal arrow. Drag the new mouse pointer into the second paragraph, immediately *after* the first sentence.

4. Position the mouse pointer and phantom insertion point to the left of the letter "T" in the word "The."

5. Release the left mouse button. Notice that the sentence is inserted at the mouse pointer, causing the existing text to wrap to the next line.

6. To remove the highlighting from the text:
   CLICK: anywhere in the unselected area of the document

7. The drag and drop method can also be used to copy text. Select the word "failures" in the first paragraph:
DOUBLE-CLICK: failures
The word should be highlighted.

8. To copy this word into the title area:
PRESS: CTRL and hold it down

9. Position the mouse pointer over the highlighted word and then drag the selection to the right of the word "SYSTEMS" in the title.

10. Release the left mouse button and then the CTRL key. Notice that Word automatically places a space between the word "SYSTEMS" and the word "failures."

11. To change the copied text to uppercase:
PRESS: SHIFT + F3 twice
The title should now read "COMPUTER SYSTEMS FAILURES."

12. Close the document and do not save the changes.

QUICK REFERENCE
Using Drag and Drop

- **To move information, select the text to move and then drag the selected text to the desired location.**
- **To copy information, select the text to copy, press CTRL and hold it down, and then drag the selected text to the desired location.**

IN ADDITION USING DRAG AND DROP BETWEEN OFFICE APPLICATIONS

The procedure for dragging and dropping between applications is identical to performing the procedure within the same document. Be-

fore initiating the drag and drop procedure, ensure that both applications (for example, Word and Excel) appear on the screen at once.

FINDING AND REPLACING TEXT

Imagine that you have just completed a 200-page proposal supporting the importation of llamas as household pets in North America. As you are printing the final pages, a colleague points out that you spelled *llama* with one *l* throughout the document. The Spell Checker didn't catch the error since both *llama*, the animal, and *lama*, the Tibetan monk, appear in Word's dictionary. Therefore, you must use another of Word's editing features—the Find and Replace utility—to correct your mistake.

The Find and Replace commands under the Edit menu allow you to search for and replace text, nonprinting characters like the Paragraph Symbol (¶), and formatting characteristics. Next you demonstrate the power of these two commands.

Perform the following steps . . .

1. Retrieve the "Hardware" document from the Advantage Files location.

2. To begin a search for a word or phrase in the document:
CHOOSE: Edit, Find
Your screen should now appear similar to Figure 3.2. (*Note*: The dialog box may look similar to Figure 3.3.)

FIGURE 3.2

FIND AND REPLACE DIALOG BOX

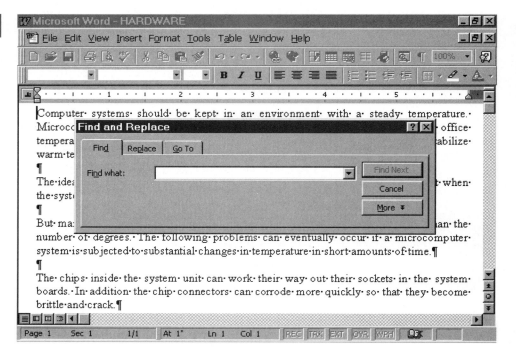

3. With the insertion point in the *Find what* text box:
TYPE: can

4. In this step, you instruct Word to only retrieve whole words. That is, you don't want Word to retrieve all words containing the letters "can" (for example, you don't want to retrieve words like *can*non or s*can*). To do this you must click the More button.
CLICK: More button
Your screen should appear similar to Figure 3.3. (*Note*: If your dialog box now looks like Figure 3.2, click the More button again.)
CLICK: *Find whole words only* check box

FIGURE 3.3

FIND AND REPLACE
DIALOG BOX:
ADDITIONAL OPTIONS
ARE DISPLAYING

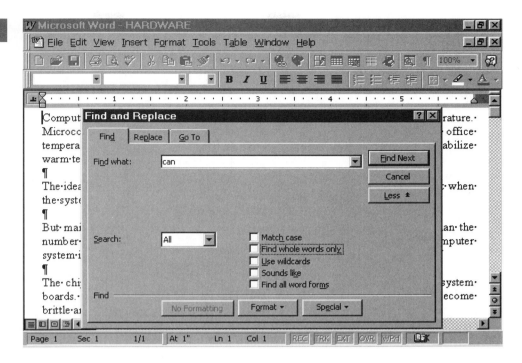

5. To tell Word to begin the search:
PRESS: **ENTER** or CLICK: Find Next

6. Word stops at the first occurrence of "can." (*Note:* You will probably need to drag the dialog box downward to see that "can" is now selected in your document.) To continue the search:
PRESS: **ENTER** or CLICK: Find Next

7. To cancel the search at this point:
CLICK: Cancel button

8. Return to the top of the document to begin a new search operation:
PRESS: **CTRL** + **HOME**

9. Let's replace the word "can" with "will" throughout the document:
CHOOSE: Edit, Replace
Notice that the word "can" already appears in the *Find what* text box from the last time we performed the Edit, Find command.

10. To enter the replacement text, you must first click the I-beam mouse pointer in the *Replace with* text box to position the insertion point.

11. TYPE: will
Your screen should now appear similar to Figure 3.4.

FIGURE 3.4

REPLACE DIALOG BOX

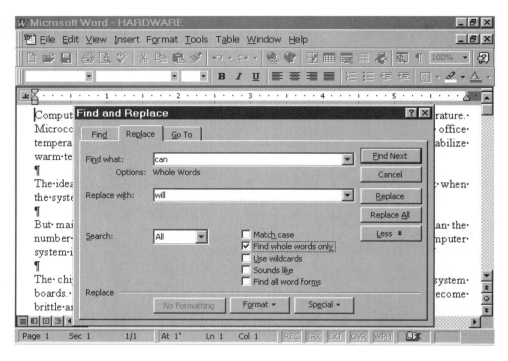

12. To execute the replacement throughout the document:
CLICK: Replace All command button
A dialog box appears informing you that four replacements were made in the document.

13. To close the dialog boxes:
PRESS: (ENTER) or CLICK: OK
CLICK: Close command button

14. Now let's make all occurrences of the word "will" bold:
CHOOSE: Edit, Replace

15. In the *Find what* text box:
TYPE: will

16. Position the insertion point in the *Replace With* text box by clicking the I-beam mouse pointer in the text box.

17. Since the word "will" already appears in this text box, you need only specify the bold formatting option. For this exercise:
CLICK: Bold button (B) on the Formatting toolbar
Notice that the formatting characteristics appear below the text box.

18. To perform the replacement:
CLICK: Replace All command button
Similar to last time, four replacements are made in the document.

19. To close the dialog boxes:
PRESS: (ENTER) or CLICK: OK
CLICK: Close button (⊠)
If you browse through the document, you will notice that all occurrences of the word "will" have been made bold.

20. Save the document as "Replaced" to the Data Files location.

21. Close the document.

QUICK REFERENCE
Finding and Replacing Text

1. CHOOSE: Edit, Find, or Edit, Replace

2. TYPE: text to find and, if necessary, the replacement text

3. To refine your search, click the More button.

4. SELECT: Find Next, Replace, Replace All, or Cancel

USING AUTOTEXT

In Session 2 you saw that by simply typing a few characters, Word will complete certain words for you, such as the months of the year. In this section, you learn more about this feature, called AutoText. With AutoText, you can store frequently used words, phrases, and even graphics, such as a company logo, for easy access. Once defined, you retrieve an **AutoText entry** by typing an abbreviated code and then pressing (F3). Word replaces the code with the full text or graphic it represents.

Perform the following steps . . .

1. Retrieve the "Sailboat" document from the Advantage Files location.

2. The company name, used quite frequently in this sample letter, is quite long and difficult to type. Therefore, it provides a perfect candidate for an AutoText entry. To define it as an AutoText entry, you begin by selecting the full text in the first sentence:
SELECT: Sam's Superior Sailboats
(*Caution*: Do not select the formatted company name that appears in the heading area.)

3. To define the selected text as an AutoText entry:
CHOOSE: Insert, AutoText
CHOOSE: New
Your screen should now appear similar to Figure 3.5.

FIGURE 3.5

AUTOTEXT DIALOG BOX

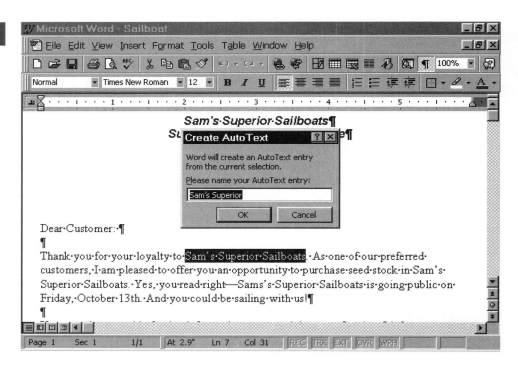

4. Although Word provides an optional name for this entry, you should enter your own abbreviation to use in retrieving the company name.
TYPE: sss
PRESS: ENTER or CLICK: OK

5. Move to the bottom of the document and try out the AutoText entry:
PRESS: CTRL + END
PRESS: Space Bar
TYPE: of sss

6. To replace the abbreviated code with the full text:
PRESS: F3

Before	*After*
Sincerely,	Sincerely,
Sam Silverton	Sam Silverton
Founder of sss	Founder of Sam's Superior Sailboats

7. You are now going to add a graphic to the AutoText library. To select the graphic at the top of the page, position the mouse pointer on the wheel and click the left mouse button once. When properly selected, the graphic appears within a framed box. The Picture toolbar automatically appears.

8. To add the graphic as an AutoText entry:
CHOOSE: Insert, AutoText
CHOOSE: New

9. Enter the following code:
TYPE: logo
PRESS: ENTER or CLICK: OK

10. Move to the bottom of the document:
PRESS: CTRL + END

PRESS: ENTER to add a new line

11. To insert the logo:
TYPE: logo
PRESS: F3
The logo appears below the text.

12. Save the document as "AutoText" to the Data Files location and then close the document.

QUICK REFERENCE
Creating an AutoText Entry

1. **SELECT: the desired text for an AutoText entry**
2. **CHOOSE: Insert, AutoText, New**
3. **TYPE: the abbreviated code for accessing the entry**
4. **PRESS: ENTER or CLICK: OK**

IN ADDITION INSERTING AUTOSHAPES

Word 97 provides AutoShapes, such as circles, stars, and banners, that you can insert and resize in your document. To insert an AutoShape:

1. CHOOSE: Insert, Picture, AutoShapes
2. SELECT: a category from the AutoShapes toolbar
3. Select a shape from the pull-down menu.
4. In your document, drag with the mouse to position and size the shape.

5. To add formatting to the object, point to it and double-click. Make selections in the Format AutoShape dialog box and then press ENTER or click OK.

6. To resize the object, point to it and click. Selection handles appear around the object. Drag a selection handle in the desired direction. (*Note*: To delete an object, point to it and click. Then press DELETE.)

USING THE SPELLING AND GRAMMAR CHECKER

Word provides the following major proofing tools: the Spelling and Grammar Checker and the Thesaurus. In this section, you use the Spelling and Grammar Checker to review a single word, a selection of text, or an entire document. In addition, you learn how to add items to the AutoCorrect feature. Below, we describe some of the spelling and grammar features that you will encounter.

Using AutoCorrect

AutoCorrect is duly named for its ability to automatically correct your typographical and capitalization errors as you type. You will find this feature extremely handy if you habitually misspell or mistype particular words. For example, people commonly type "thier" instead of "their"—knowing perfectly well how to spell the word but making a simple typing mistake. By adding this word to the AutoCorrect list, you can have Word correct this error automatically.

Correcting Spelling Errors

Word can perform a spelling check automatically as you type (Word's default setting) or all at once if you click the Spelling and Grammar button (ABC) on the Standard toolbar. When Word performs a spelling check, it begins by comparing each word to entries in Word's main dictionary, which contains well over 100,000 words. If a word cannot be found, the Spelling Checker attempts to find a match in a custom dictionary that you may have created. Custom dictionaries usually contain proper names, abbreviations, and technical terms.

When you use the Spelling and Grammar button (ABC) to correct a document's spelling, a dialog box appears when the Spelling Checker cannot identify a word and believes it to be misspelled. The Spelling Checker also flags errors relating to repeated words (for example, "the ball was was red") and mixed case (for example, "the baLL was rEd"). The Spelling and Grammar dialog box provides options for correcting or ignoring the entry and for adding words to the custom dictionary or to the AutoCorrect feature.

Correcting Grammar Errors

Word contains grammatical rules and style considerations for every occasion. Word offers the following styles of grammar checking: Casual, Standard (the default setting), Formal, Technical, and Custom. You can also customize Word to check only for specific rules and wording styles. The procedure for correcting grammar errors is almost identical to the one for correcting spelling errors.

Another feature of the Grammar Checker is the **readability statistics** dialog box (Figure 3.6) that can appear at the completion of the spelling and grammar check. By default, it doesn't appear. You can select to display it by choosing Tools, Options and then selecting *Show readability statistics* in the *Spelling & Grammar* tab. Besides counting the number of words, the Readability Statistics dialog box measures the readability of a document, basing its scores on the number of words per sentence and the average number of syllables per word.

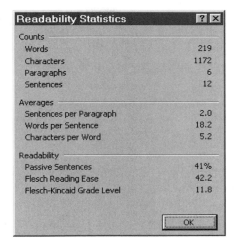

FIGURE 3.6

READABILITY STATISTICS
DIALOG BOX: "SPELLING"
DOCUMENT

In this section you practice using the Spelling and Grammar button ([ABC]) on the Standard toolbar.

Perform the following steps . . .

1. Retrieve the "Spelling" document from the Advantage Files location. This document is a copy of the "Hardware" document with several intentional typographical errors and misspellings.

2. To start a spelling check:
   CLICK: Spelling and Grammar button ([ABC])
   (*Note*: You can also start a spelling check by choosing the Tools, Spelling and Grammar command.) When Word finds the first misspelled word, it displays a dialog box (Figure 3.7) and waits for further instructions.

FIGURE 3.7

SPELLING AND GRAMMAR
DIALOG BOX

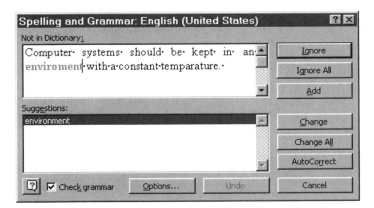

3. You have several options when the Spelling and Grammar Checker cannot find a word in its dictionary or detects a grammar error:
   - If a word is misspelled and the proper version appears in the *Suggestions* list box, highlight the word in the list box and click the Change or Change All buttons. You should consider adding the word to the Auto-Correct feature as well.

- If the word is misspelled and none of the suggestions is correct, type the proper version into the *Not in Dictionary* text box and then click the Change or Change All buttons. You should consider adding the word to the AutoCorrect feature as well.

- If the word is spelled correctly and not frequently used, click the Ignore or Ignore All buttons to proceed to the next word.

- If the word is spelled correctly and frequently used, click the Add button to add it to the custom dictionary.

- If a grammar error is detected and the proper grammar appears in the *Suggestions* list box, highlight the word in the list box and click the Change button.

- If a grammar error is detected and none of the suggestions is correct, type the proper version into the text box, located on the top of the dialog box, and then click the Change button.

- If a grammar error detected by Word is actually correct grammar, click the Next Sentence button to continue.

To correct the misspelled word "enviroment," ensure that the correct spelling of the word appears in the *Suggestions* text box and then:
CLICK: Change command button

4. The next word that the Spelling Checker finds is "temparature." Let's add this word to the AutoCorrect feature. Make sure the correct spelling of the word appears in the *Suggestions* text box and then do the following:
CLICK: AutoCorrect command button

5. The next word that the Spelling Checker finds is "Farenheit." Make sure the correct spelling of the word (Fahrenheit) appears in the *Suggestions* text box and then do the following:
CLICK: Change command button

6. Word has now detected a grammar error. Your screen should appear similar to Figure 3.8. The dialog box shows the offending phrase and suggests why it was flagged. Word thinks you should delete the comma (,) after "Operating." To accept this suggestion:
CLICK: Change command button

FIGURE 3.8

SPELLING AND GRAMMAR
DIALOG BOX: CHECKING
THE GRAMMAR

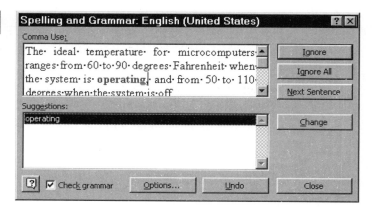

7. On your own, continue the spelling and grammar check for the rest of the document. A message dialog box will appear when it is finished. To clear this dialog box:
PRESS: (ENTER) or CLICK: OK
(*Note*: If the Readability Statistics dialog box appears, press (ENTER) or click OK again.)

8. The Word Count command is another useful tool that provides some basic document statistics. To display the Word Count dialog box:
CHOOSE: Tools, Word Count

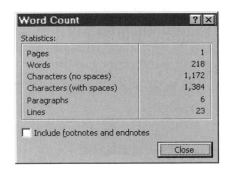

9. To close the Word Count dialog box:
PRESS: (ENTER) or CLICK: Close

10. Save the document as "Spelling-Done" to the Data Files location.

11. Close the document.

QUICK REFERENCE
Using the Spell and
Grammar Checker

1. **CLICK: Spelling and Grammar button (🔤), or**

2. **CHOOSE: Tools, Spelling and Grammar**

3. **When a misspelled word is found, you can accept Word's suggestion, change the entry, ignore the word and the suggested alternatives provided by Word, or add the term to the AutoCorrect feature or custom dictionary. When a grammar error is detected you can accept Word's suggestion, change the entry, or ignore the sentence.**

USING THE THESAURUS

Have you ever found yourself with the "perfect" word at the tip of your tongue—only to have it stay there? This situation is not limited to authors and professional writers. In fact, most people experience this sensation whenever they sit down to set their thoughts on paper. Fortunately, Word provides a helping hand with its built-in **Thesaurus.** A thesaurus provides quick access to synonyms (words with similar meanings) and antonyms (words with opposite meanings) for a given word or phrase. You invoke Word's Thesaurus utility by choosing Tools, Language, Thesaurus from the menu or by pressing (SHIFT) + (F7).

In this section, you choose a synonym.

Perform the following steps . . .

1. Retrieve the "Hardware" document from the Advantage Files location.

2. Using the mouse, select the word "steady" at the end of the first sentence in the first paragraph.

3. CHOOSE: Tools, Language, Thesaurus
Your screen should now appear similar to Figure 3.9.

FIGURE 3.9

THESAURUS DIALOG BOX

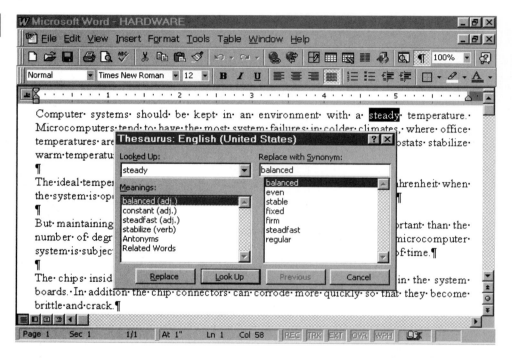

4. Since a word may have several interpretations, you can select the appropriate meaning from the *Meanings* list box. The *Replace with Synonym* list box displays the synonyms for the highlighted meaning. You have three options available after selecting a word from the *Replace with Synonym* list box:

   - Select the Replace command button to replace the word in the document with the highlighted word.

   - Select the Look Up command button to display additional synonyms for the highlighted word.

   - Type a word into the *Replace with Synonym* text box and then select the Look Up or Replace command buttons.

   To change the word "steady," select the word "stable" in the *Replace with Synonym* list box and then do the following:
   SELECT: Replace command button

5. Let's find a synonym for the word "ideal," appearing near the beginning of the first sentence in the first paragraph. To begin, select the word "ideal."

6. PRESS: (SHIFT) + (F7)

7. In the *Replace with Synonym* list box:
SELECT: perfect

8. To look up synonyms for "perfect":
CLICK: Look Up command button

9. To display the previous list of synonyms:
CLICK: Previous command button

10. To replace the word "ideal," select the word "perfect" in the *Replace with Synonym* list box and then do the following:
CLICK: Replace command button

11. Close "Hardware" without saving.

QUICK REFERENCE
Using the Thesaurus

1. Select a word to look up in the Thesaurus.

2. CHOOSE: Tools, Language, Thesaurus or PRESS: (SHIFT) + (F7)

3. Select the desired word in the *Replace with Synonym* list box.

4. SELECT: Replace command button

IN ADDITION INSERTING COMMENTS

When a document is produced as part of a collaborative effort, it is important that you are able to insert comments directly into the document. To do this in Word:

1. Display the Reviewing toolbar.

2. In the Word document, select the text that you want to comment on.

3. CLICK: Insert Comment button ( ) on the Reviewing toolbar

4. TYPE: a comment into the bottom half of the document window

5. CLICK: Close command button

Word highlights words that have an associated comment and, as you move the I-beam pointer over the highlighted text, the comment appears above.

Summary

This session focused on Word's editing and proofing tools. After a discussion on working with multiple document windows, the session described two methods for copying and moving information: using the Clipboard and using drag and drop. You also used the Find and Replace commands to search for and replace text and formatting in a document. The section on AutoText demonstrated how easy it is to insert frequently used text and graphics into a document by typing abbreviated codes. The last half of this session concentrated on proofing documents using the Spelling and Grammar Checker and the Thesaurus.

Table 3.2 provides a list of the commands covered in this session.

TABLE 3.2

Command Summary

Task Description	Menu Command	Toolbar Button	Keyboard Shortcut
Select a window to make active	Window, *document name*		
Size and display all open document windows	Window, Arrange All		
Create a new window view for the active document	Window, New Window		
Copy the selected text to the Clipboard	Edit, Copy	🖻	CTRL + c
Move the selected text to the Clipboard	Edit, Cut	✂	CTRL + x
Insert or paste the Clipboard's contents	Edit, Paste	📋	CTRL + v
Find text in a document	Edit, Find		CTRL + f
Find and replace text in a document	Edit, Replace		CTRL + h
Create an AutoText entry	Insert, AutoText		
Retrieve an AutoText entry			F3
Perform a spelling and grammar check of a document	Tools, Spelling and Grammar	ᴬᵇᶜ	F7
Display a list of synonyms for the selected word	Tools, Language, Thesaurus		SHIFT + F7
Count the number of words in a document	Tools, Word Count		

KEY TERMS

AutoText entry

A frequently used text or graphic that is inserted into a document by typing an abbreviated code and then pressing F3 .

Clipboard

In Windows, the Clipboard is a program that allows you to copy and move information within an application or among applications.

drag and drop

A feature of Windows that allows you to copy and move information by dragging objects or text from one location to another using the mouse.

readability statistics
A statistics page appears after the Grammar Checker has completed its check; provides a grade-level reading equivalency for a document.

Thesaurus
In Microsoft Word, a proofing tool that provides synonyms and antonyms for the selected word or phrase. A synonym is a word that has the same meaning as another word. An antonym has the opposite meaning.

EXERCISES

SHORT ANSWER

1. How many windows can be open in the document area at one time?

2. How do you move between open documents using the mouse?

3. What are the two methods for copying and moving information? How do they differ?

4. Name three types of information that can be searched for using the Find command.

5. How do you create an AutoText entry?

6. How do you insert an AutoText entry?

7. Explain what you would do if the Spell Checker came across a frequently used word that is correctly spelled but Word cannot find it in its main dictionary.

8. How is the Thesaurus tool used?

9. Besides counting words, what other statistics appear in the Word Count dialog box?

10. How are grade levels awarded for the readability statistics?

HANDS-ON

(*Note*: Ensure that you know the location of your Advantage Files and where to store your Data Files. If necessary, ask your instructor or lab assistant for additional information.)

1. The objective of this exercise is to practice performing copy and move operations using the Clipboard and drag and drop methods.

   a. Create the document appearing in Figure 3.10.

FIGURE 3.10

"ORDERS" LETTER

Alpha Beta Computer Rentals
5900 Algonquin Road
Suite 775
Ashton, NC 28804

September 3, 1997

Ms. Lolita Balfour
2910 Freemont Road
Raleigh, NC 27610

Dear Ms. Balfour:

Thank you for your order! I am writing to confirm
that the following items will be delivered to your
premises on September 25th.

Items Shipped

MONITOR: TLC SVGA Color Monitor
OPTIONS: 28.8K Baud Internal Fax/Modem
HARD DISK: MaxStore 1.6 GB Hard Drive
CPU: Compact Pentium 100 with 32MB RAM
VIDEO CARD: ABC Ultrasonic Graphics Card

Yours truly,

your name
Accounts Representative

P.S. If I can be of any assistance, please call me
at 704-250-9987.

b. Save the document as "Orders" to your Data Files location.

c. Using the Clipboard, move the text after "P.S." (starting at the word "If") above the line "Yours truly." Leave the "P.S." at the bottom of the letter.

d. Using the Clipboard, move the first sentence in the first paragraph ("Thank you for your order!") after the "P.S." on the last line.

e. Using the drag and drop method, change the order of the Items Shipped to the following: CPU, HARD DISK, MONITOR, VIDEO CARD, OPTIONS.

f. Using the drag and drop method, copy the company name "Alpha Beta Computer Rentals" from the top of the page to below the title "Accounts Representative" in the closing.

g. Save the document again, replacing the original version.

h. Print the document.

i. Close the document.

2. This exercise gives you practice using AutoText entries and the Find and Replace commands.

a. Open a new document.

b. Enter the following information at the top of the page, substituting your name and address for the italicized text shown below:

your name
your address
your city, state   zip code

c. Define one AutoText entry for all of the text, using your initials as the abbreviated code.

d. PRESS: **ENTER** twice

e. TYPE: `Management Information Systems Department`

f. Define an AutoText entry called MIS for this term. (*CAUTION*: Do not select the paragraph mark, just the text.)

g. PRESS: **ENTER** twice

h. TYPE: `OS/2 Version 2.2 Batch Release 2.299`

i. Define an AutoText entry called OS for this term. (*CAUTION*: Do not select the paragraph mark, just the text.)

j. Open a new document.

k. Create the document appearing in Figure 3.11, using the AutoText entries wherever possible.

FIGURE 3.11

"MIS DEPARTMENT"
MEMO

DATE: February 14, 1997

TO: Mr. Tyler French
             Director of Operations
             Management Information Systems Department

FROM: *your name*
             your address
             your city, state zip code

SUBJECT: OS/2 Version 2.2 Batch Release 2.299

Please be forewarned that the OS/2 Version 2.2
Batch Release 2.299 operating system will not be
available for the Management Information Systems
Department on March 1, 1997, as previously promised.

Although we understand the requirement for OS/2
Version 2.2 Batch Release 2.299, Research and
Development must fully test the product before
allowing any department access to the code—and that
includes the Management Information Systems
Department.

If you require further clarification, please have
Alan Johansen, V.P., Management Information Systems
Department, contact me at the following address:

    your name
    your address
    your city, state zip code

Thanks for your patience.

---

l. Save the document as "MIS Department" to the Data Files location.

m. Using the Replace command, change the name of the department from "Management Information Systems Department" to "Office Automation Division."

n. Using the Replace command, make every occurrence of "OS/2 Version 2.2 Batch Release 2.299" boldface in the document.

o. Save the document again, replacing the original version.

p. Print the document.

q. Close all the open documents in the document area. Do not save the original document that you used to define the AutoText entries.

3. The following exercise uses the proofing tools to correct a poorly written and misspelled document.

   a. Retrieve the "Badmemo" document from the Advantage Files location.

   b. Correct the misspelled words and grammar errors with the help of the Spelling and Grammar Checker.

   c. Save the document as "Goodmemo" to the Data Files location. (*Note*: You will need to choose File, Save As if you are saving to a different disk.)

   d. Print the document.

   e. Close the document.

4. The objective of this exercise is to practice move operations using the Clipboard, Find and Replace commands, the Thesaurus tool, and the Spelling and Grammar Checker.

   a. Open "Input" from the Advantage Files location.

   b. Using the Clipboard, change the order of the hardware components to match the following: pen-based computing, touch screen, digitizer, mouse, trackball, light pen.

   c. Using the Replace command, change every occurrence of "computer" to "PC." (*Note*: Make sure that you select the *Find whole words only* check box.)

   d. Use the Thesaurus to find a different word for "Essentially" in the first sentence of the Trackball description.

   e. Correct the misspelled words with the help of the Spelling and Grammar Checker.

   f. Save the document as "Input Hardware" to the Data Files location. (*Note*: You will need to choose File, Save As if you are saving to a different disk.)

   g. Print the document.

   h. Close the document.

5. On your own, describe your hobby. In a 1- to 2-page document, describe your current hobby or favorite pursuit. Create a formatted cover page that includes the title for your document, your name, and the current date. Create an AutoText entry for your name and the current date. Using the AutoText feature, include your name and the current date in the closing of the document. Check your document for spelling and grammar errors before saving the document. Save the document as "On Your Own-5" to your Data Files location and then print the document.

6. On your own, design a flyer that describes an upcoming event, such as an auto show or school picnic. The objective of the flyer is to get the word out about the event and to motivate people to attend. Include your name at the end of the flyer as the contact person for the event. Check your document for spelling and grammar errors before saving the document. Save the flyer as "On Your Own-6" to your Data Files location and then print the flyer. *Extra Credit*: Add special text effects to the flyer using WordArt.

CASE PROBLEMS | **THE *RIVER REPORT***

(*Note*: In the following case problems, assume the role of the primary characters and perform the same steps that they identify. You may want to re-read the session opening.)

1. Linda's first task as editor for the *River Report* is to edit a short article written about a big bass caught in the Sacramento River. Billy Joe Quaker, the staff reporter, left the following note on her desk:

    Dear Ms. James, I saved the bass article as "Bass" in the Advantage Files location. The article was written using Microsoft Word for Windows. If you need me, I'll be at Chatterbox Falls covering the kayaking race. Bye for now, BJQ.

    Upon reviewing Billy Joe's article, Linda decides that some of the sentences should be positioned differently and that the spelling and grammar must be checked. When finished, she saves the document to her Data Files location and then prints it for inclusion in the Sports section.

2. At 5:00 P.M. on Wednesday, reporter Tola McPherson submitted her article about Saturday's baseball game. The article is named "Baseball" and is stored in the Advantage Files location. As it is one of the first articles that Linda has had to review, she doesn't know what to expect when she opens the document. She is pleasantly surprised, however, because the article seems relatively error-free. To be on the safe side, however, Linda runs the document through Word's Spelling and Grammar Checker and implements its suggestions where appropriate.

    Sounding embarrassed, Tola calls Linda at 5:45 P.M. to tell her to change the name "Collin Lamas" to "Victor Lamas." Linda swiftly makes the change using Word's Replace command. Now that she has put her stamp of approval on the article, she saves it to her Data Files location and sets it aside until Thursday evening, when she will give it to Production.

3. As Linda is organizing the articles to give to Production, Tola rushes in with a last-minute change. "Linda, I have some very interesting information about Victor Lamas and I think we need to include it in our 'Baseball' article. The information is stored in a file named 'Lamas' in the Advantage Files location. I've gotta run to follow up on a lead." With 6:00 P.M. appearing on

her desk clock, Linda knows that she doesn't have much time to make the changes! She opens the "Baseball" document from the Data Files location into one window and the "Lamas" document from the Advantage Files location into another. After reading both documents, she decides to move the first paragraph from the "Lamas" document and position it immediately after the second paragraph in the "Baseball" document. She then moves the second paragraph from the "Lamas" document and positions it after the last paragraph in the "Baseball" document.

Satisfied with the revised "Baseball" document, Linda saves "Baseball" to her Data Files location and prints her work at 6:30 P.M. She just makes the 7:00 P.M. deadline!

4. As tradition would have it, a complimentary ad is published each year in the *River Report* announcing the upcoming Pear Fair on June 15th. Linda is responsible for creating the advertisement. To begin, she reviews some of the previous document files left by Hank Leary. Fortunately, she finds a file named "Pearfair" stored in the Advantage Files location. After opening the file, she is even more comfortable with the task at hand. Hank had included bracketed notes throughout the document to help him create the advertisement for this year's fair.

    Linda reviews the document and incorporates all of Hank's suggestions. She then deletes each of his bracketed notes from the document. After saving the document as "Pearfair-Final" to her Data Files location, she prints it for inclusion in the Special Events section.

5. Linda must write a short article describing the 4th of July parade. She attended the parade and jotted down some notes that are now stored in "Parade" in the Advantage Files location. But the notes are rough and were not placed in a particular order. Therefore, she must edit and move around the text to form a legible paragraph. Also, she has since learned that Bruce Towne drove the fire engine, not Bill Darsie. She can fix that mistake using the Replace utility. As a final step, she corrects the spelling and grammar. She saves the document to her Data Files location as "Parade-Final" and prints it for inclusion in the Special Events section.

Microsoft Word 97 for Windows

Printing and Document Management

SESSION OUTLINE

INTRODUCTION

After the final editing and proofing of a document, there remain only a few optional steps for finalizing its appearance. Some of these steps include specifying the page layout, preventing widows and orphans, inserting page numbers, and creating headers and footers; each helps to keep your audience on track when reading your document. This session also introduces several printing and file management commands. To work efficiently with a word processing software program, it is important that you know how to find, copy, and print a document without having to open each file stored on your hard disk. This session provides you with the knowledge and experience to perform these functions confidently.

GINO'S PIZZA KITCHEN

Gino Lerma is the owner of four pizza restaurants in the Boston metropolitan area. He started with one restaurant 15 years ago and, through hard work and careful planning, Gino was able to open a new restaurant every few years. Gino now considers himself semi-retired, even though he works around the clock and requires a full-time assistant, Larry Ingla. Although he is no longer part of the daily activities, Gino fondly remembers his many years working until midnight, six days per week, in the restaurants.

Each month, Gino's managers use Microsoft Word to create a summary report of their restaurant's activities. Each manager then sends his or her report to Larry Ingla. Larry uses the Windows Clipboard to create a single document from the four reports and then prints the consolidated report for Gino to review. With feedback from his bank manager on the consolidated reports, Gino has asked Larry to format the reports with headers, footers, and page numbers. He also wants Larry to improve the general page layout of the reports and has given him specific suggestions for improvement. Larry immediately agreed to Gino's request, but in truth, he doesn't know where to begin.

In this session, you and Larry will learn how to take control of the way your document appears on the screen and when printed, how to use document formatting commands, and how to manage the files you create using several file management commands.

CUSTOMIZING YOUR WORK AREA

Microsoft Word has many advantages over character-based word processing programs like WordPerfect 5.1. Not only can you see the effects of character and paragraph formatting commands immediately on-screen, you can also edit text using features such as drag and drop. One of the disadvantages of working in this WYSIWYG environment is that it may take longer to page through a document on-screen. For example, Word must continuously update the screen with all of the special fonts and graphics that you have selected, unlike a character-based program which simply displays basic characters. Since most people haven't learned how to type faster than the computer can think, this last point may be a little academic.

As a compromise, Word provides four primary views for working with documents: Normal, Online Layout, Page Layout, and Outline. While each view has its own advantages, it is their combination that gives you the best overall working environment. For faster data entry, you can also select a Draft Font for the Normal and Outline views. Since the Draft Font presents text without WYSIWYG formatting, the screen is updated and redrawn as fast as most character-based word processing programs. This section describes and demonstrates the Normal, Online Layout, and Page Layout views.

SELECTING A VIEW

You select a view for your document using the View command on the Menu bar or by clicking the desired View button on the horizontal scroll bar. On the pull-down menu, a bullet appears next to the active or currently selected view. Table 4.1 summarizes the view options.

TABLE 4.1

View Options

Task Description	Menu Command	View Button
Change to Normal view	View, Normal	
Change to Online Layout view	View, Online Layout	
Change to Outline view	View, Outline	
Change to Page Layout view	View, Page Layout	

Your selection of a view depends upon the type of work that you are performing, as described in the following guidelines:

- *Perform most of your work using the Normal view.*
  The Normal view displays text with character and paragraph formatting, but does not show headers, footers, or newspaper-style text columns. The Normal view separates pages in a document with a dotted line, dividing the last line of one page from the first line of the next. Figure 4.1 shows a sample document in the Normal view.

FIGURE 4.1

A DOCUMENT DISPLAYED
IN NORMAL VIEW

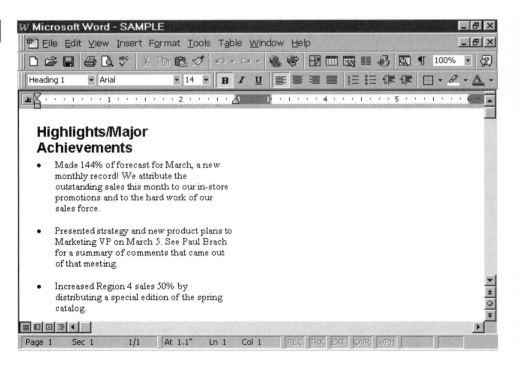

- *Read a document on the computer screen in Online Layout view.*
  The Online Layout view is optimized for reading on screen. The document appears in a larger font and with more space in between lines. The page layout is determined based on the computer screen rather than by the paper. Also, by default Word displays a separate pane called the *document map* in Online Layout view. You use the document map to navigate your document. Figure 4.2 shows a document in Online Layout view.

FIGURE 4.2

A DOCUMENT DISPLAYED
IN ONLINE LAYOUT VIEW

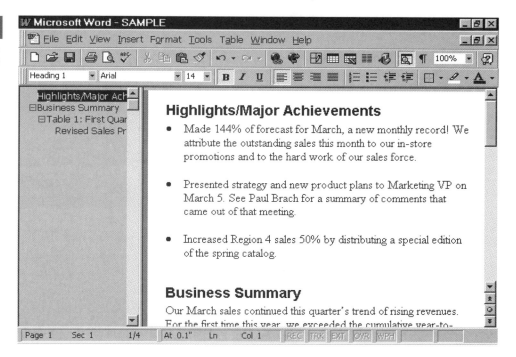

- *Edit the final document before printing in the Page Layout view.*
  The Page Layout view displays a document in almost full WYSIWYG preview mode. All character, paragraph, and document formatting options are displayed, along with headers, footers, and newspaper-style text columns. The document is separated on-screen into what appear to be real pages. Figure 4.3 shows a document in the Page Layout view.

FIGURE 4.3

A DOCUMENT DISPLAYED
IN PAGE LAYOUT VIEW

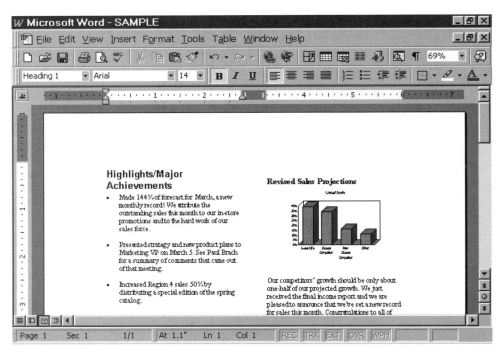

- *Organize and plan your document using the Outline view.*
  The Outline view displays a document as an outline with expandable and
  collapsible heading levels. This view is used for rearranging entire sections
  of a document or for moving to a specific section in a long document
  quickly. Figure 4.4 shows a document in the Outline view, collapsed to show
  only the major headings.

FIGURE 4.4

A DOCUMENT DISPLAYED
IN OUTLINE VIEW

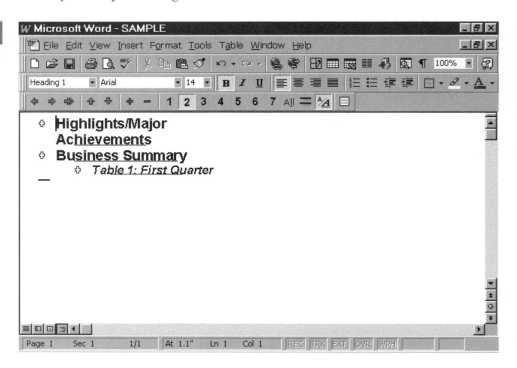

● *Enter large amounts of text quickly using the Draft Font.*
The Draft Font mode speeds up the display of a document by not showing
WYSIWYG character formatting. Although you continue to select the
desired formatting, the formatted text only appears underlined in the document. You select the *Draft Font* check box by choosing Tools, Options from
the Menu bar and then clicking the *View* tab. Figure 4.5 displays a document in Normal view and Draft Font.

FIGURE 4.5

A DOCUMENT DISPLAYED
IN NORMAL VIEW AND
DRAFT FONT

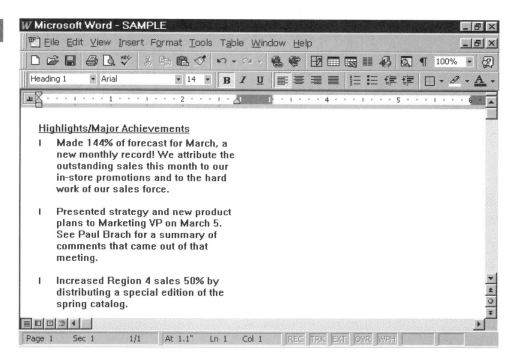

● *Work with the largest text area possible using Full Screen mode.*
The Full Screen mode lets you work on a document without
the clutter of Word's Menu bar, toolbars, or Ruler. Indeed, the
only indication that you are still using Word is the Full Screen
button (shown at right) that appears in the document area. To change to Full
Screen mode, choose View, Full Screen from the menu. To return to the
regular Word workspace once you are in Full Screen mode, choose Close
Full Screen from the Full Screen button or press [**ESC**].

In this section you practice selecting different views.

**Perform
the
following
steps . . .**

1. Retrieve the "Newsltr" document from the Advantage Files location.

2. To change to a Page Layout view:
CHOOSE: View, Page Layout
Your screen should now appear similar to Figure 4.6.

FIGURE 4.6

THE "NEWSLTR"
DOCUMENT IN PAGE
LAYOUT VIEW

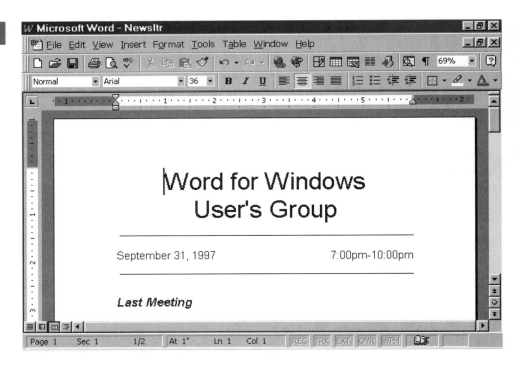

3. To change to Full Screen mode:
CHOOSE: View, Full Screen
You may be asking, "How do I choose commands if Word removes the
Menu bar and toolbars?" In Full Screen mode, you must use the keyboard
shortcut keys and shortcut (right-click) menus. (*Tip:* You can sometimes
access the Menu bar by pointing to the very top of the screen and clicking
the left mouse button.)

4. To return to the regular Word workspace:
PRESS: (**ESC**) or SELECT: Close Full Screen in the Full Screen box

5. Now let's change to Online Layout view:
CHOOSE: View, Online Layout
Your screen should appear similar to Figure 4.7.

FIGURE 4.7

THE "NEWSLTR"
DOCUMENT IN
ONLINE LAYOUT VIEW

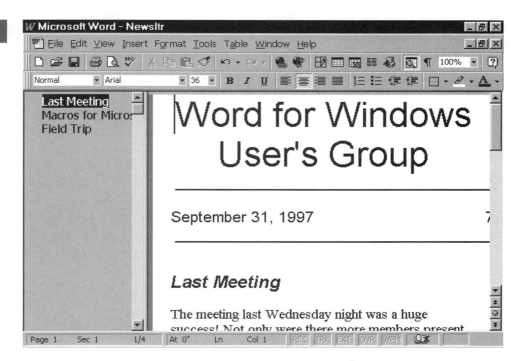

6. You can move to other parts of the document by clicking in the document map, the pane located on the left. To illustrate:
   CLICK: "Macros for Micros" in the left pane
   As you can see, the cursor moved to the new location.

7. If you work with documents that contain many headings and subheadings, you should know that you can expand and collapse the headings in the document map. For example:
   RIGHT-CLICK: a document heading in the document pane
   With the menu that appears you can select which headings appear in the document map. This document contains only main headings (Heading 1).

8. To return to the document without making a selection:
   CLICK: in the document area

9. You can also change the background color to enhance your online viewing. Any color you choose appears only in Online Layout view. To illustrate:
   CHOOSE: Format, Background
   CLICK: the color of your choice

10. To change back to the Normal view:
    CHOOSE: View, Normal
    Notice that the background color you chose in the previous step doesn't appear in Normal view.

11. Now let's change to the Draft Font:
    CHOOSE: Tools, Options
    CLICK: *View* tab
    SELECT: *Draft Font* check box in the *Show* area
    Your screen should now appear similar to Figure 4.8.

FIGURE 4.8

OPTIONS DIALOG BOX
WITH DRAFT FONT
SELECTED

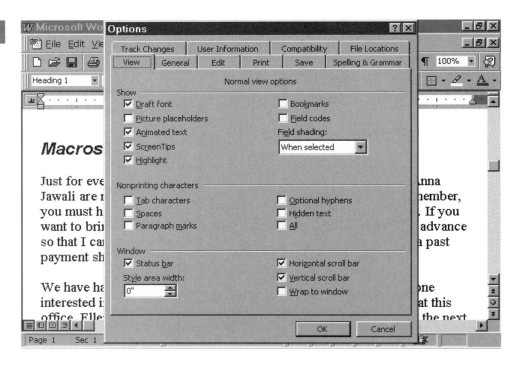

12. To return to the document:
PRESS: (**ENTER**) or CLICK: OK
You should notice that the document changes to an almost character-based display.

13. To remove the Draft display mode:
CHOOSE: Tools, Options
SELECT: *Draft Font* until no "✓" appears in the check box
PRESS: (**ENTER**) or CLICK: OK

14. To move to the top of your document:
PRESS: (**CTRL**) + (**HOME**)

QUICK REFERENCE

Selecting a View

- **For a normal WYSIWYG view:**

  CLICK: Normal button (▤)

- **For a WYSIWYG display that includes a document map:**

  CLICK: Online Layout button (▣)

- **For a full WYSIWYG display:**

  CLICK: Page Layout button (▤)

- **For a collapsible outline view:**

  CLICK: Outline button (▤)

ZOOMING THE DISPLAY

Regardless of the view you select, Word lets you zoom in and out on a document, increasing and decreasing its display size. For example, you may want to enlarge Word's normal view to 200% of its original size when working with detailed graphics. To modify Word's zoom setting, you choose the View, Zoom command or select the Zoom Control box ([100% ▾]) on the Standard toolbar.

Let's demonstrate how to zoom the display.

 **Perform the following steps . . .**

1. To zoom the "Newsltr" document to 200% its original size:
   CLICK: down arrow beside the Zoom Control box ([100% ▾])

2. From the resulting drop-down list:
   SELECT: 200%
   The document is immediately magnified twice its original size.

3. To find the best-fit magnification:
   CLICK: down arrow beside the Zoom Control box ([100% ▾])
   Your screen should now appear similar to Figure 4.9.

FIGURE 4.9

ZOOMING THE DISPLAY
USING THE ZOOM
CONTROL BOX

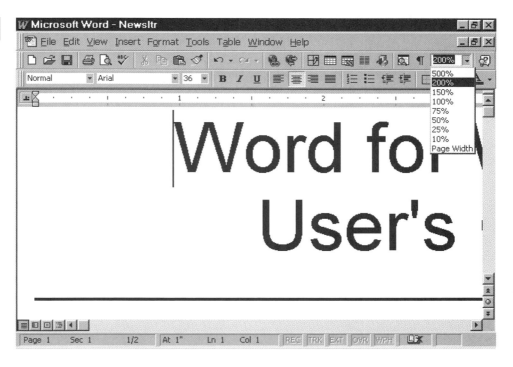

4. SELECT: Page Width from the drop-down list
   The view is zoomed to the best fit for your screen's resolution.

5. In addition to using the Zoom Control box ([100% ▾]) to select a magnification factor, you can use the Zoom dialog box:
   CHOOSE: View, Zoom
   Your screen should now appear similar to Figure 4.10.

FIGURE 4.10

ZOOM DIALOG BOX

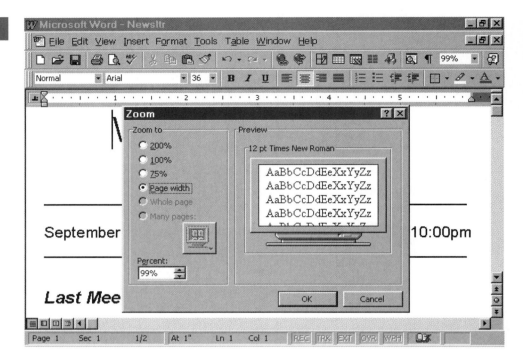

6. SELECT: the various magnification options in the *Zoom to* area
Notice that the text displayed on the monitor in the *Preview* area is updated after each selection.

7. Before you proceed to the next section:
SELECT: Page Width
PRESS: **ENTER** or CLICK: OK

DISPLAYING AND HIDING TOOLBARS

Another method for customizing the work area involves manipulating the toolbars in Word. Most people work with only the Standard and Formatting toolbars displayed. However, you can open the additional eleven toolbars (AutoText, Control Toolbox, Database, Drawing, Forms, Picture, Reviewing, Tables and Borders, Visual Basic, Web, and WordArt) and move them anywhere within the application window. Don't get carried away and display all of the toolbars on the screen at all times. You should attempt to keep your screen as clear as possible to maximize your document's work area.

Let's demonstrate some of the features that are available for manipulating toolbars.

Perform the following steps . . .

1. To display the shortcut or pop-up menu for accessing toolbars, position the mouse pointer on any button in the Standard toolbar and click the right mouse button once. The shortcut menu on page 141 should appear.

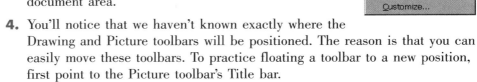

2. To display the Drawing toolbar:
   CHOOSE: Drawing
   Remember to click the command using the left mouse button. You should see the Drawing toolbar appear, usually positioned at the bottom of the screen. (*Note*: You can also display the Drawing toolbar by clicking the Drawing button (🖉) on the Standard toolbar.)

3. To display the Picture toolbar using the Menu bar:
   CHOOSE: View, Toolbars
   SELECT: Picture
   The Picture toolbar will appear somewhere in the document area.

4. You'll notice that we haven't known exactly where the Drawing and Picture toolbars will be positioned. The reason is that you can easily move these toolbars. To practice floating a toolbar to a new position, first point to the Picture toolbar's Title bar.

5. CLICK: left mouse button and hold it down
   DRAG: the toolbar to the right side of the document window
   You should notice that the shadowed frame changes from a horizontal bar to a vertical bar.

6. Now drag the Picture toolbar back to the center of the screen. Do this by pointing to the line that separates two buttons and then dragging the toolbar to the center.

7. To make the Picture toolbar appear more compact, drag the bottom border of the Picture toolbar downward. The toolbar on your screen may appear similar to the example at right.

8. Using the shortcut menu, remove the Drawing and Picture toolbars from the screen.

9. One last item for customizing your work area—you can hide the Ruler to create more screen real estate using the following command:
   CHOOSE: View, Ruler

10. To re-display the Ruler:
    CHOOSE: View, Ruler

QUICK REFERENCE
Customizing Your Work Area

- **To zoom in or out on your document:**
  CHOOSE: View, Zoom, or click the Zoom Control box (100% ▾)
- **To display or hide toolbars:**
  CHOOSE: View, Toolbars, or right-click a toolbar to display a menu
- **To display or hide the Ruler:**
  CHOOSE: View, Ruler

DOCUMENT FORMATTING COMMANDS

Simply stated, document formatting involves preparing a document for the printer. This section provides lessons on setting margins, specifying paper sizes and orientation, preventing widows and orphans, inserting page numbers, and lastly, creating headers and footers in a document.

SPECIFYING YOUR PAGE LAYOUT

Your document's page layout is affected by many factors, including the margins or white space desired around the edges of the page, the size of paper you are using, and the print orientation. Fortunately for us, Word provides a single dialog box for controlling all of these factors. Accessed by choosing File, Page Setup from the menu, the Page Setup dialog box provides four tabs: Margins, Paper Size, Paper Source, and Layout. Figure 4.11 shows the Page Setup dialog box with the *Margins* tab selected. The entry areas for the other three tabs are provided below the dialog box.

FIGURE 4.11

PAGE SETUP DIALOG
BOX: MARGINS TAB

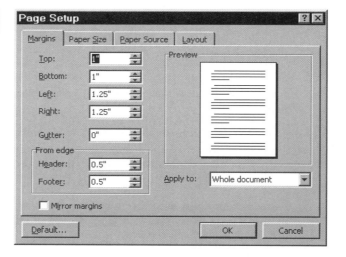

 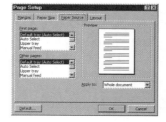 

Not surprisingly, Word allows you to set the top, bottom, left, and right margins for a page. In addition, you can set a gutter margin to reserve space for binding a document. The **gutter** is where pages are joined in the center of the binding or hole-punched for a ring binder. Word provides default settings of 1.25 inches for the left and right margins and 1 inch for the top and bottom margins. The gutter margin is initially set at 0 inch, as most documents are not bound. With respect to paper size, typical options include using letter- or legal-sized paper with a **por-trait orientation** (8.5 inches wide by 11 inches tall) or a **landscape orienta-tion** (11 inches wide by 8.5 inches tall). For the purposes of this section, you will not modify the paper source or section layout options.

Let's now practice changing the page layout settings.

Perform the following steps . . .

1. Close all the open documents in the document area without saving.

2. Retrieve the "Proposal" document from the Advantage Files location.

3. To change the margins from the default settings to an even 1 inch around the entire page:
   CHOOSE: File, Page Setup

4. Ensure that you are viewing the margin settings:
   CLICK: *Margins* tab

5. To change the left and right margins to 1 inch:
   CLICK: down triangle beside the *Left margin* text box repeatedly, until the value decreases to 1 inch
   CLICK: down triangle beside the *Right margin* text box repeatedly, until the value decreases to 1 inch
   (*Note*: As you click the symbols, the *Preview* area at the right-hand side shows the effect of the change on your document.)

6. To illustrate the use of a gutter, you will increase the counter in the *Gutter* text box to 0.5 inch:
   CLICK: up triangle beside the *Gutter* text box repeatedly, until the value increases to 0.5 inch
   (*Note*: The shaded area in the *Preview* area represents the binding.)

7. Reset the Gutter margin to 0 inch.

8. To select legal-size paper with a landscape orientation for this document, first display the paper size and orientation information:
   CLICK: *Paper Size* tab

9. SELECT: Legal 8½ × 14-in from the *Paper Size* drop-down list

10. SELECT: *Landscape* option button from the *Orientation* area
    Notice that the *Preview* area changes with each selection.

11. PRESS: (**ENTER**) or CLICK: OK

12. When you return to the document, the page may be too wide to fit in the current view. To remedy this problem:
    CLICK: Page Layout button (▣)
    CLICK: Zoom Control box (100% ▾)
    CHOOSE: Page Width
    Your screen should now appear similar to Figure 4.12.

FIGURE 4.12

PAGE LAYOUT VIEW
WITH A LANDSCAPE
ORIENTATION

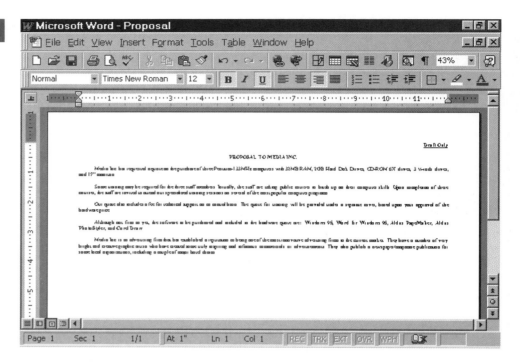

13. To return the document to letter-size paper with a portrait orientation, you will call up the Page Setup dialog box using a shortcut method:
DOUBLE-CLICK: gray area in the Ruler (see diagram below)

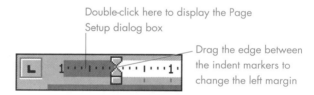

Double-click here to display the Page Setup dialog box

Drag the edge between the indent markers to change the left margin

14. When the Page Setup dialog box appears:
CLICK: *Paper Size* tab
SELECT: Letter 8½ × 11-in from the *Paper Size* drop-down list
SELECT: *Portrait* option button from the *Orientation* area
PRESS: **ENTER** or CLICK: OK
The document is immediately redrawn in the Page Layout view.

15. To change a document's margins using the mouse, you position the mouse pointer over the margin boundary (the line between the gray area and the white area on the Ruler) and then drag the boundary to increase and decrease the margin setting. (See the diagram in step 13.) If you've positioned your mouse pointer correctly, it changes from a white arrow to a black, two-headed arrow. To have Word display the margin measurements in the Ruler as you drag the margin boundary, you hold down the **ALT** key.

Let's proceed—do the following:

PRESS: (**ALT**) and hold it down

DRAG: left margin boundary to the right until 1.3 appears as the measurement on the horizontal Ruler

(*Note*: In Normal view, the double-headed arrow doesn't appear.) Your screen should now appear similar to Figure 4.13.

FIGURE 4.13

CHANGING MARGINS IN
PAGE LAYOUT VIEW
USING THE MOUSE
AND (**ALT**) KEY

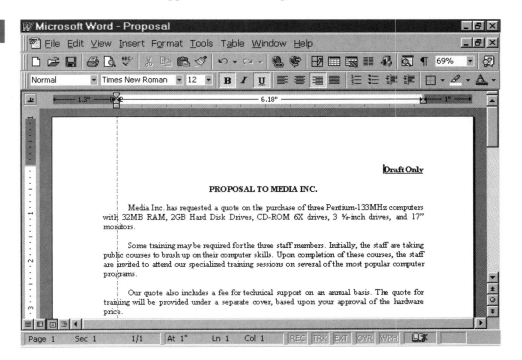

16. Release the mouse button and the (**ALT**) key.

17. Using the same method as outlined in step 16, change the right margin to 1.3 inches. (*Note*: You can use this same method to change left, right, top, and bottom margins in a document.)

18. Save the document as "Proposal-Revised" to the Data Files location. (*Note*: If you are saving to a different disk you will need to use the File, Save As command.)

19. Close the document.

QUICK REFERENCE

Using the Page Setup
Dialog Box

1. **CHOOSE: File, Page Setup**
2. **CLICK:** *Margins* **tab to display the settings page for margins**
3. **Specify a gutter margin if binding the document, as well as the top, bottom, left, and right margins.**
4. **CLICK:** *Paper Size* **tab**
5. **Specify the paper size and either portrait or landscape orientation.**

PREVENTING WIDOWS AND ORPHANS

Although the heading implies a plan for abolishing family suffering, this section deals with a much less serious topic—straggling sentences that are separated from their paragraphs by a page break. A **widow** is created when the last sentence in a paragraph flows to the top of the next page. An **orphan** is created when the first sentence of a paragraph begins on the last line of a page. When a single sentence is separated from a paragraph, the reader must work harder to keep up with the flow of the text. Fortunately, Word has a widow and orphan protection feature that automatically prevents these breaks from occurring.

In this section, you check the widow/orphan settings on your computer.

Perform the following steps . . .

1. Retrieve the "Newsltr" document from the Advantage Files location.

2. To ensure that the Widow and Orphan protection feature is turned on:
   CHOOSE: Format, Paragraph
   The Paragraph dialog box appears.

3. CLICK: *Line and Page Breaks* tab

4. Under the Pagination group, ensure that the *Widow/Orphan Control* check box is selected:
   SELECT: *Widow/Orphan Control* check box
   Remember, a "✓" in the check box means that the option is selected.

5. PRESS: ENTER or CLICK: OK

QUICK REFERENCE
Protecting Against Widows and Orphans

1. **CHOOSE: Format, Paragraph**
2. **CLICK: *Line and Page Breaks* tab**
3. **SELECT: *Widow/Orphan Control* check box in the *Pagination* area**
4. **PRESS: ENTER or CLICK: OK**

INSERTING PAGE NUMBERS

Page numbers assist a reader in finding and referencing sections within a document. In Word, you can position page numbers at the top or bottom of a document and align the page number with the left, center, or right margins. Furthermore, you can select the format and starting page for the numbering scheme based on personal preference. For example, you can use standard numbers (1, 2, 3 . . .), letters (a, b, c . . . or A, B, C . . .), or Roman numerals (i, ii, iii . . .) for the numbering format and change the format for different sections in a document.

To add page numbers to a document, you choose the Insert, Page Numbers command. When the Page Numbers dialog box appears, you specify the position and alignment desired for the page numbers. Depending on your selections, Word creates a header or footer using the default numbering format (1, 2, 3 . . .), starting at page 1.

Let's now demonstrate how to insert page numbers.

Perform the following steps . . .

1. CHOOSE: Insert, Page Numbers
The dialog box in Figure 4.14 should appear on your screen. (*Note*: Figure 4.14 also shows the dialog box for changing the numbering format from standard numbers to letters or Roman numerals.)

FIGURE 4.14

PAGE NUMBERS DIALOG BOX

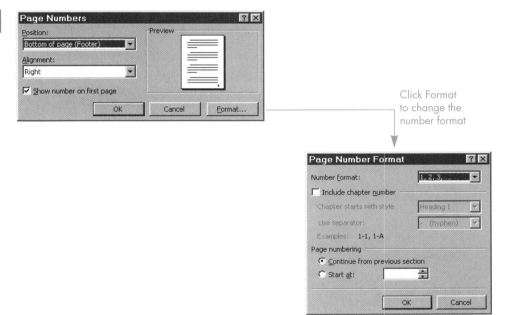

Click Format to change the number format

2. To position the page number in the bottom right-hand corner of the page:
SELECT: Bottom of Page (Footer) in the *Position* drop-down list box
SELECT: Right in the *Alignment* drop-down list box

3. PRESS: **ENTER** or CLICK: OK
Word automatically changed the view to Page Layout view.

4. To see the page number on the bottom of Page 1, you're going to first position the cursor on the top of Page 2 and then press the (⬆) key.
DRAG: the horizontal scroll box to the top of Page 2
CLICK: in the heading (Field Trip) of page 2
PRESS: (⬆)
In the bottom right-hand corner, a "1" appears as the page number.

5. To change back to the Normal view:
CLICK: Normal button (▤)

Because Word places the page numbering scheme into the header or footer of a document, you can further customize the page numbers by selecting a font and style for them.

1. **CHOOSE: Insert, Page Numbers**
2. **SELECT: an option from the *Position* drop-down list box**
3. **SELECT: an option from the *Alignment* drop-down list box**
4. **PRESS: ENTER or CLICK: OK**

CREATING HEADERS AND FOOTERS

A document **header** and **footer** appear at the top and bottom of each page. The header often contains the title or section headings for a document while the footer might show the page numbers or copyright information. Adding a header or footer produces a more professional-looking document and makes longer documents easier to read.

In the last section, you inserted page numbers in the "Newsltr" document. When you specified that the numbering should appear at the bottom of the page, Word automatically created a header for the document. To view the page numbers, you switched to Page Layout view since headers and footers are not visible in Normal view. In the next exercise, you learn how to edit and format the header in Page Layout view.

In this section, you create a footer.

Perform the following steps . . .

1. Make sure that the "Newsltr" document is open in the document area.

2. To edit the header and footer for the "Newsltr" document:
CHOOSE: View, Header and Footer
Upon choosing this command, Word switches you to Page Layout view, displays the Header and Footer toolbar, creates a framed editable text area for the header and footer, and dims the document's body text. Your screen should now appear similar to Figure 4.15. Figure 4.16 identifies the buttons in the Header and Footer toolbar.

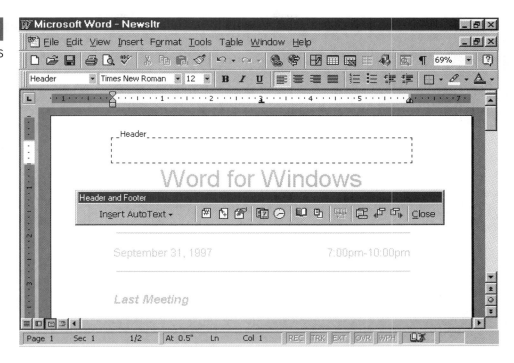

3. Let's leave the header area unchanged. To view the footer:
CLICK: Switch Between Header and Footer button (▣) on the Header and
Footer toolbar

4. The page number, inserted last section, appears at the far right-hand side of
the first line in the footer area. Your insertion point should appear flashing
at the left edge. Let's now enter information about when the document was
last printed.
TYPE: **Printed on**
PRESS: Space Bar

5. To place the date and time in the footer and have them automatically updated when you print the document:
CLICK: Insert Date button (🖻) on the Header and Footer toolbar
PRESS: Space Bar
TYPE: at
PRESS: Space Bar
CLICK: Insert Time button (🕓) on the Header and Footer toolbar

6. To format this new title, you must first select the text:
SELECT: Printed on (current date) at (time)
SELECT: Arial from the *Font* drop-down list (Times New Roman ▾)
SELECT: 10 point from the *Font Size* drop-down list (10 ▾)
CLICK: Bold button (**B**)
(*Note*: If the Arial font isn't available on your computer, choose a different font.)

7. As in the previous step, you format the page number by first selecting the text. However, Word places the page number in a special box called a frame. To select text inside a frame, you must position the I-beam pointer carefully and drag across the text. Do not drag the mouse pointer when it appears as a pointer with a cross-shaped, four-headed arrow—this moves the entire frame.

Now, do the following:
DRAG: I-beam mouse pointer across the page number
The page number should appear highlighted and surrounded by a shaded box (see below).

(*Note*: An anchor may also appear to the left of the framed text box indicating that the page number is anchored to the right border of the footer. Anchors are used when framing text and graphics, a topic beyond the scope of this guide.)

8. To format the page number with the same options as the title:
SELECT: Arial from the *Font* drop-down list (Times New Roman ▾)
SELECT: 10 point from the *Font Size* drop-down list (10 ▾)
CLICK: Bold button (**B**)
Congratulations, you've finished creating and formatting the footer! Your screen should now appear similar to Figure 4.17 (with a different date and time in the footer, of course).

FIGURE 4.17

COMPLETED FOOTER FOR
THE "NEWSLTR"
DOCUMENT

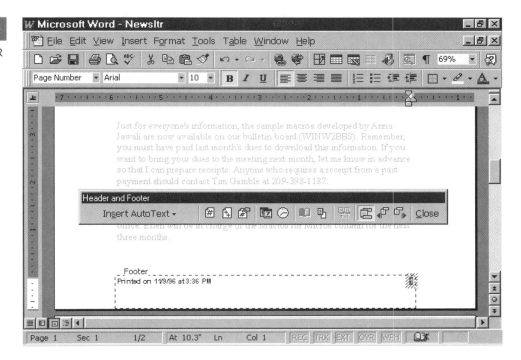

9. To finish editing the footer and return to your document:
CLICK: Close button (Close) on the Header and Footer toolbar
You are returned to the view you were using prior to choosing the View, Header and Footer command.
(*Tip*: You can double-click the dimmed body text in the Page Layout view to return to editing the document. To switch back to the header and footer in Page Layout view, you double-click its dimmed text.)

10. Ensure that you are viewing the document in Normal view:
CLICK: Normal button (▤)

11. Save the document as "Footer Exercise" to the Data Files location. (*Note*: If you are saving to a different disk, you will need to use the File, Save As command.)

QUICK REFERENCE
Creating a Header or Footer

1. **CHOOSE: View, Header and Footer**
2. **Edit and format the header and footer using the regular formatting commands and the buttons on the Header and Footer toolbar.**
3. **CLICK: Close button (Close)**

IN ADDITION WORKING WITH TEMPLATES

If your proposals, for example, all use the same margin settings, headers and footers, character formatting commands, and perhaps display the company logo on the top of the page, consider creating a template that stores all the elements that you typically include in a document proposal.

A *template* is a file that contains all the parts and features of a particular type of document. A template can contain text, headers, footers, graphics, page and paper layouts, and more.

For more information, choose Help, Contents and Index. Click the *Index* tab, and then type `templates` to display a list of topics.

PRINTING A DOCUMENT

This section introduces the printing commands for Word, including setting print options and previewing the output. The Windows Printers folder provides a centralized location for tasks relating to printing, including installing a new printer, changing printer settings, and checking or changing the status of scheduled print jobs. You access the Printers folder from the taskbar by clicking the Start button and then choosing Settings, Printers.

To coordinate the printing of multiple documents, Windows places documents temporarily in a print spooler or **queue** on the hard disk. When the printer has completed one print job, Windows takes the next print job from the queue and feeds it to the printer. Because this spooling process occurs in the background, you can continue working in an application immediately after you send a document to the printer. The Windows print spooler is a full 32-bit application, which means you realize little or no slow-down when you send a document to the printer.[1] In other words, there is no waiting for the printer to complete its work before you can continue your own work.

PREVIEWING THE DOCUMENT

A primary benefit of working with today's sophisticated word processing programs, including Word, is the ability to preview documents in a full-page display before sending them to the printer. To access Word's Print Preview mode, you choose File, Print Preview from the menu or click the Print Preview button (▣) on the Standard toolbar. Some of the features of Print Preview include the following:

- View one page (▣) or multiple pages (▦) at the same time.
- Select Zoom mode to view your document or Edit mode to modify and format your document without leaving Print Preview.
- Make last minute changes to margin settings by dragging the margin boundaries on the Ruler, similar to Page Layout view.

---

[1]In Windows 3.1, print spooling was handled by the Print Manager program.

Let's demonstrate how to preview a document.

Perform the following steps . . .

1. Make sure that the "Footer Exercise" document is open in the document area.

2. CLICK: Print Preview button ( )
   Upon selecting this command, Word switches you to Print Preview mode. Your screen should now appear similar to Figure 4.18. Figure 4.19 identifies the buttons on the Print Preview toolbar.

FIGURE 4.18

PREVIEWING THE "FOOTER EXERCISE" DOCUMENT

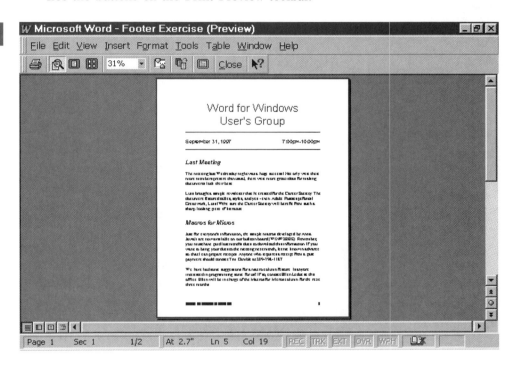

FIGURE 4.19

PRINT PREVIEW TOOLBAR

3. To zoom in on the document, move the mouse pointer over the first paragraph until it changes to a magnifying glass with a plus sign.

4. CLICK: left mouse button once to zoom the view to 100%
   Notice that the plus sign in the magnifying glass mouse pointer changes to a minus sign.

5. To switch Print Preview from Zoom mode to Edit mode:
   CLICK: Magnifier button ( )

6. Move the mouse pointer over the document. Notice that the mouse pointer becomes an I-beam, as opposed to a magnifying glass.

7. To format the title text:
SELECT: Word for Windows

8. To display the shortcut menu for formatting text:
RIGHT-CLICK: the selected text
CHOOSE: Font

9. In the Font dialog box:
SELECT: 48 point from the *Size* list box
SELECT: Bold from the *Font Style* list box
PRESS: (**ENTER**) or CLICK: OK

10. To change back to Zoom mode:
CLICK: Magnifier button ([🔍])

11. To zoom out, position the magnifying glass mouse pointer over the document and click the left mouse button once.

12. To exit Print Preview:
CLICK: Close button ([Close])

13. Save the "Footer Exercise" document to the Data Files location, replacing the original version.

QUICK REFERENCE
Previewing a Document

1. **CLICK: Print Preview button ([🔍])**

2. **Use Zoom mode to view the document and Edit mode to change margin settings, edit text, and format your document.**

3. **CLICK: Close button ([Close]) to return to the document**

IN ADDITION KEEPING LINES TOGETHER

After previewing a document, you may decide that you don't want a page break to appear in the middle of a paragraph:

1. CHOOSE: Format, Paragraph

2. CLICK: *Line and Page Breaks* tab

3. SELECT: *Keep Lines Together* check box

PRINTING THE DOCUMENT

If you are satisfied with your document after viewing it in Page Layout view and Print Preview, it's time to send it to the printer. The quickest and easiest method for printing a single copy of every page in a document is to click the Print button ([🖨]) on the Standard toolbar. If you want to print specific pages only, or if you want multiple copies of a document, you must choose the File, Print command and make your selections in the Print dialog box (shown in Figure 4.20).

FIGURE 4.20

PRINT DIALOG BOX

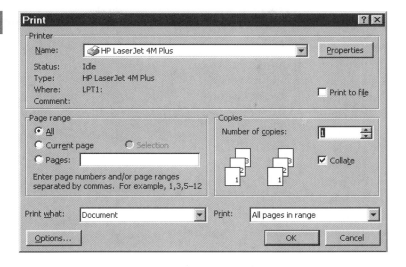

Perform the following steps . . .

1. To print the "Footer Exercise" document:
   CLICK: Print button (🖨)
   You will see a small printer icon appear in the Status bar as the document is sent to the printer. If you wanted to cancel the print job (which you don't in this exercise), you could double-click this printer icon or press **ESC**.

2. Close all the documents in the document area.

QUICK REFERENCE
Printing a Document

1. **CLICK: Print button (🖨)**
2. **Select the number of copies to print, and specify whether to print certain pages or the entire document.**
3. **PRESS: ENTER or CLICK: OK**

IN ADDITION CREATING A POWERPOINT SLIDE SHOW FROM A WORD DOCUMENT

Don't think that you're limited to a printer when outputting your Word documents. For example, you can easily output your Word document to PowerPoint which can turn it into a slide presentation. PowerPoint creates slides based on the heading styles you've used in your document. A *heading style* is formatting that you apply to a heading. Word comes with nine different heading styles, labeled Heading 1 through Heading 9. (In Word, you select styles from the Style menu on the Formatting toolbar.) The title of each slide is created from text formatted with the Heading 1 style, the next level of text on each slide is created from text formatted with the Heading 2 style, and so on.

To create a PowerPoint presentation from a Word outline:

1. Open the document in Word for which you want to create a PowerPoint presentation.

2. CHOOSE: File, Send To

3. CHOOSE: Microsoft PowerPoint

For more information, choose Help, Contents and Index. Click the *Contents* tab and select the "Sharing Information with Other Users and Applications" topic. Then explore the "Sharing Text, Data, and Graphics" topic.

FILE MANAGEMENT COMMANDS

While creating, formatting, and printing documents are definitely major topics in this guide, the importance of file management should not be understated. Without file management commands, you could not back up your work, free up disk space for more files, or organize your documents into a logical filing system. Specifically, file management refers to copying, moving, deleting, renaming, and sorting documents that reside on your hard disk and floppy diskettes.

CREATING A DOCUMENT INVENTORY

Most of Word's file management utilities can be accessed through the Open dialog box. While primarily a document retrieval tool, you can also print, preview, copy, delete, rename, sort, and search for files. In addition, you can create a shortcut to a document on the Windows desktop and send a file to an e-mail or fax recipient. This section provides an example of how you can use the Open dialog box to search for documents and change how files are viewed.

In this section, you locate files and change the document view.

Perform the following steps . . .

1. Ensure that there are no open documents in the document area.

2. CLICK: Open button (🖼)

3. To display the types of files that you can search for:
   CLICK: down arrow beside the *Files of type* text box (near the bottom of the dialog box)

From this drop-down list, you can limit your search to Word Documents, Document Templates, Rich Text Format files, Text files, or many other types of files. Or, you can perform a broad search for All Files. You can also type in your own file specification if you want to search for specific files not included in the drop-down list.

4. SELECT: Word Documents from the *Files of type* drop-down list

5. To have Word search the Advantage Files location for Word Documents:
CLICK: down arrow beside the *Look in* text box
SELECT: *your Advantage Files location*
All of the Word Document files in the Advantage Files location will appear in the file list area. (*Note*: This same procedure can be used to search an entire hard disk.)

6. To narrow the search to files that begin with the characters "Gino":
CLICK: *File name* text box
TYPE: Gino
CLICK: Find Now button
Five files should appear in the file list area.

7. To refresh the search criteria:
CLICK: New Search button
All of the Word Document files in the Advantage Files location again appear in the file list area.

8. There are four views available in the Open dialog box. Each can be accessed using the Open dialog box toolbar.

- List (⊞)　　　　　　　Displays folder and filenames with small icons.

- Details (▦)　　　　　　Displays standard file information, including the document's name, size, type, and the date it was last modified.

- Properties (⊞)　　　　Displays a summary screen for the highlighted file, containing document statistics, comments, and other useful information.

- Preview (⊞)　　　　　Displays a preview of the highlighted file in the list.

To display a preview of a document file:
SELECT: "Software" document in the file list area
CLICK: Preview button (⊞)
Your screen should now appear similar to Figure 4.21.

FIGURE 4.21

PREVIEWING A
DOCUMENT

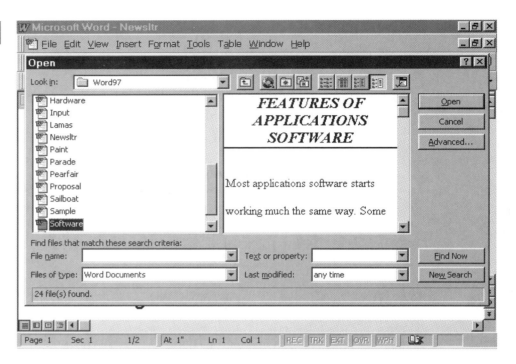

9. To display all the files in the Advantage Files location in the Details view:
CLICK: Details button (▥)

10. To display the files in a list view:
CLICK: List button (▤)

11. To sort the list by file size, you use the Commands and Settings button in
the Open dialog box toolbar. Do the following:
CLICK: Commands and Settings button (⬚)
CHOOSE: Sorting

12. CLICK: down arrow beside the *Sort files by* text box
SELECT: Size from the drop-down list
PRESS: **ENTER** or CLICK: OK button
The list is sorted in ascending order by file size. (*Hint*: You can also click
the column headings in the Details view to sort documents in the file list
area. Click the heading twice to switch between ascending and descending
order.)

13. On your own, sort the files in ascending order by the filename.

14. To close the Open dialog box:
CLICK: Cancel button

1. **CLICK: Open button (🖼)**

2. **To change the view, click the List (▦), Detail (▦), Properties (▦), or Preview button (▦).**

3. **To change the sort order, click the Commands and Settings button (🖼) and then choose the Sorting command.**

MANAGING INDIVIDUAL FILES

Besides displaying and opening files, the Open dialog box provides commands for copying, moving, renaming, and deleting files. These file management tasks are among the most common performed in word processing. The Copy and Cut commands enable you to copy or move a file to a new drive or directory. The Rename command renames the selected file, and the Delete command removes the file from the current drive or directory.

Another useful feature is the ability to select more than one file at a time for copying, moving, deleting, and printing documents. There are two methods for selecting a group of documents.

First, to select a group of contiguous files (all files are next to each other in the list box), you select the first file, hold down the (SHIFT) key, and then click the last file. All the documents between the first and last files are automatically highlighted. Second, to select a group of noncontiguous files, you select the first file and then hold down the (CTRL) key while clicking on each additional file. Once the files are highlighted, you right-click with the mouse to issue a file management command from the shortcut menu.

In this section, you copy a file to the hard disk, delete the copied file, and then rename a file.

Perform the following steps . . .

1. CLICK: Open button (🖼)

2. To place a copy of the "Newsltr" document on the hard disk, point to the file and then right-click with the mouse.

3. CHOOSE: Copy

4. You will copy the "Newsltr" file to the root directory of the hard disk (drive C:) and then delete it later. Do the following:
   CLICK: down arrow beside the *Look in* drop-down list box
   SELECT: the icon that represents drive C:

5. To paste the document into the root directory of drive C:
   RIGHT-CLICK: an empty area in the file list area
   CHOOSE: Paste
   A dialog box appears briefly informing you that the file is being copied. Although this example teaches you how to copy files from drive A: to drive C:, you are more likely to copy files from your hard disk to a diskette in order to back up your documents.

6. To delete the "Newsltr" file from drive C:, point to the file and then right-click with the mouse.

7. CHOOSE: Delete
SELECT: Yes when asked to confirm the deletion (see below)

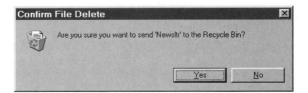

(*Note*: Word provides another method for deleting a file. After you select a file, you can delete it by pressing the **DELETE** key.)

8. Before renaming a file in the next step, change the search path back to the Advantage Files location:
CLICK: down arrow beside the *Look in* drop-down list box
SELECT: *your Advantage Files location*

9. To change the name of the "Gino1996" document to "1996Gino," point to the "Gino1996" document and then right-click with the mouse.

10. CHOOSE: Rename
TYPE: `1996Gino`
A text editor box still appears around the new name.

11. To remove the text editor box:
PRESS: **ENTER**

12. On your own, rename the "1996Gino" document back to its original name (Gino1996).

13. To close the Open dialog box:
CLICK: Cancel button

QUICK REFERENCE
Copying and Deleting Files

1. **CLICK: Open button (🖼)**
2. **Copy, cut (move), delete, or rename a file by pointing to the file and right-clicking with the mouse. You then choose the appropriate command from the shortcut menu that appears.**

PRINTING FILES

Word allows you to print one document or multiple documents directly from the Open dialog box. As in the process for copying and deleting files, you highlight the desired file or files, right-click with the mouse, and then choose the Print command. When the Print dialog box appears, you specify the number of copies you want printed and then press **ENTER** or click OK.

Perform the following steps . . .

1. CLICK: Open button ()
   The files in the Advantage Files location should appear.

2. To print both the "Newsltr" and "Proposal" documents, first select the files from the file area:
   SELECT: "Newsltr" in the file area

3. Position the mouse pointer over the "Proposal" document.

4. PRESS: CTRL and hold it down
   CLICK: left mouse button once
   Both files should now be highlighted.

5. Release the CTRL key.

6. Point to one of the selected files and then right-click with the mouse.

7. CHOOSE: Print
   Both documents are sent to the printer and the document screen reappears.

QUICK REFERENCE
Printing Documents

1. **CLICK: Open button ()**
2. **Print a file by pointing to it, right-clicking with the mouse, and then choosing the Print command.**

CREATING A DOCUMENT SHORTCUT

If you frequently use a particular document file, you might consider placing a shortcut to the file on the Windows desktop. Shortcuts are used to open a file or program quickly. After you load Windows, you simply double-click the shortcut on the Windows desktop to open Word and then the document. You can create a shortcut using the shortcut menu in the Open dialog box.

Perform the following steps . . .

1. CLICK: Open button ()
   CLICK: down arrow beside the *Look in* drop-down list box
   SELECT: *your Advantage Files location*
   The files in the Advantage Files location should appear.

2. Let's say that you use the "Newsltr" file often. To create a shortcut for this file, first point to the file with the mouse and then do the following:
   RIGHT-CLICK: "Newsltr" file
   CHOOSE: Create Shortcut
   A shortcut icon named "Shortcut to Newsltr" is created.

3. To copy the shortcut to the desktop, point to the shortcut file and then right-click with the mouse.

4. CHOOSE: Copy
   CLICK: Cancel button to exit the Open dialog box

5. Before you paste the shortcut onto the desktop, minimize Word so that you can see the desktop. The Windows desktop appears.

6. To paste the shortcut onto the desktop:
RIGHT-CLICK: an empty area on the desktop
CHOOSE: Paste
CLICK: an empty area of the desktop to remove the highlighting
Your screen should now appear similar to Figure 4.22.

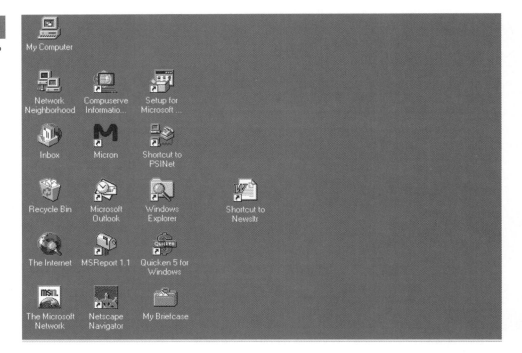

7. To test the shortcut:
DOUBLE-CLICK: "Shortcut to Newsltr" icon on the desktop
After a few moments, Word will load and the "Newsltr" document should appear in the document window.

8. Exit Word.

9. The Windows desktop appears. To delete the shortcut from the desktop, point to the shortcut and then right-click with the mouse.

10. CHOOSE: Delete
CLICK: Yes command button

QUICK REFERENCE
Creating a Shortcut

1. **CLICK: Open button (🖃)**
2. **Point to the file for which you want to create a shortcut and then right-click with the mouse.**
3. **CHOOSE: Create Shortcut**
4. **To move the shortcut to the desktop, point to the shortcut and right-click with the mouse.**
5. **CHOOSE: Cut**
6. **CLICK: Cancel button to display the document screen**
7. **CLICK: Minimize button (🔲) in the application window's Title bar**
8. **To paste the shortcut onto the desktop, point to an empty area on the desktop and right-click with the mouse.**
9. **CHOOSE: Paste**

SUMMARY

This session introduced the document formatting commands for preparing a document to send to the printer. The majority of page layout options are selected from the Page Setup dialog box, including margins, paper size, print orientation, and paper source. Other formatting topics covered this session included preventing widows and orphans, inserting page numbers, and creating headers and footers. Because the WYSIWYG capabilities of Word can sometimes slow the text entry process, Word provides several alternative views for a document. Whereas the Normal view is used for the majority of your work, you'll find that the Online Layout, Page Layout and Outline views provide additional features for finalizing and managing documents.

The second half of the session examined printing options and file management commands. Topics included using the Zoom and Edit modes in Word's Print Preview and using the Open dialog box to find, copy, delete, rename, and print documents. You also learned how to create a document shortcut and then move the shortcut to the Windows desktop. Table 4.2 provides a list of the commands and procedures covered in this session.

TABLE 4.2

Command Summary

Task Description	Menu Command	Toolbar Button	Keyboard Shortcut
Display text with character and paragraph formatting only	View, Normal	🔳	
Display text with the document map pane	View, Online Layout	🔳	
Display text with all formatting (headers, footers, and columns)	View, Page Layout	🔳	

TABLE 4.2 Continued	Task Description	Menu Command	Toolbar Button	Keyboard Shortcut
	Display a document as a collapsible outline	View, Outline	🗒	
	Access the Zoom dialog box	View, Zoom	100% ▾	
	Display or hide Word's toolbars	View, Toolbars		
	Display or hide the Ruler line	View, Ruler		
	Set page layout options	File, Page Setup		
	Set paragraph pagination options (widows and orphans)	Format, Paragraph, Line and Page Breaks tab		
	Insert page numbers in the header or footer of a document	Insert, Page Numbers		
	Change to Page Layout view for editing the header and footer	View, Header and Footer		
	Display a document in Print Preview mode	File, Print Preview	🔍	
	Send a document to the printer	File, Print	🖨	CTRL+p
	Perform file management functions	File, Open	📂	

KEY TERMS

footer
Descriptive text that appears at the bottom of each page in a document. The footer usually contains page numbers or copyright information.

gutter
The gutter is where pages are joined together in a bound document.

header
Descriptive text that appears at the top of each page in a document. The header usually contains titles or section headings.

landscape orientation
Describes how a page is printed. Letter-size paper with a landscape orientation measures 11 inches wide by 8.5 inches high. Legal-size paper with a landscape orientation measures 14 inches wide by 8.5 inches high.

orphan
In printing, a single sentence that appears at the bottom of a page, separated from the rest of its paragraph on the next page.

portrait orientation

Describes how a page is printed. Letter-size paper with a portrait orientation measures 8.5 inches wide by 11 inches high. Legal-size paper with a portrait orientation measures 8.5 inches wide by 14 inches high.

queue

In printing, a program that uses memory and the disk to line up and prioritize documents waiting for printer time.

widow

In printing, a single sentence that appears at the top of a page, separated from the rest of its paragraph on the previous page.

EXERCISES

SHORT ANSWER

1. When might you want to create a document shortcut?
2. When would you use the Draft Font?
3. How do you return to Word's application window when you are in Full Screen mode?
4. Name the four tabs in the Page Setup dialog box.
5. How do you prevent widows and orphans in a document?
6. What are two methods for inserting page numbers?
7. What are two methods for changing the margins in a document?
8. How do you preview a document before sending it to the printer?
9. What are the two modes available in Print Preview?
10. Name two methods for selecting multiple files in the Open dialog box.

HANDS-ON

(*Note*: Ensure that you know the location of your Advantage Files and where to store your Data Files. If necessary, ask your instructor or lab assistant for additional information.)

1. This exercise uses some character and paragraph formatting commands, as well as document formatting commands. Open "Software" from the Advantage Files location and then perform the following steps:

   a. Include a header that displays the current date in the flush right position.

   b. Ensure that the document is protected against widows and orphans.

   c. Left-justify the entire document.

   d. Include your name and the current page number in a footer.

   e. Check the spelling and grammar in the document.

f. Save the file as "Software" to the Data Files location. (*Remember*: If you are saving to a different disk, you will need to choose File, Save As.)

g. Print the document.

h. Close the document.

2. The following exercise retrieves an existing file from the Advantage Files location and modifies its page layout settings.

a. Retrieve "Bedford" from the Advantage Files location.

b. Change to a Page Layout view.

c. Using the Zoom Control box, shrink the display until you can see the entire page on the screen.

d. Access the Page Setup dialog box by double-clicking the Ruler.

e. Change the top, bottom, left, and right margins to 1.5 inches.

f. Using the mouse, change all the margins to 1.2 inches by dragging the margin boundaries.

g. Add a footer to the letter that centers the following phrase: "From the Desk of *your name*." Substitute your own name for the italicized words.

h. Format the footer with an Arial typeface (or another typeface on your computer) and a 10-point font size.

i. Close the footer area and return to the Normal view.

j. View the document using Print Preview.

k. Using the mouse in Print Preview, change the top and bottom margins to 1 inch.

l. Send the document to the printer from the Print Preview screen.

m. Save the document as "Bedford - Reference" to the Data Files location. (*Remember*: If you are saving to a different disk, you will need to choose File, Save As.)

n. Print the document.

o. Close the document.

3. This exercise creates a document with headers and footers.

a. Open a new document.

b. Center the title "Budget Forecast - 1997" at the top of the page.

c. Center the subtitle "ABC Realty Inc." on the next line immediately below the title.

d. Enhance the title with an Arial, 18-point font and make it bold. (*Note*: Use another font if Arial doesn't exist on your computer.)

e. Enhance the subtitle with an Arial, 14-point font and make it bold and italic.

f. Enter four blank lines and left-justify the new paragraph.

g. Make sure that the font is Times New Roman, 12 point, before proceeding.

h. Type the text appearing in Figure 4.23.

FIGURE 4.23

"BUDGET 1997"
DOCUMENT

Introduction

Now that we are in the first quarter of 1997, it is time we stopped to review our direction for the remainder of the year. We had a tough year in 1996, but it seems that the economy is well on its way to recovery. We are anticipating a good year for all the staff.

This report is confidential and should not be circulated outside of this office. It is intended to be a planning document for the Sales Team in 1997. Any questions or suggestions can be directed to your immediate supervisor.

i. Return to the top of the document.

j. Create a header and footer for the document. Center-align the text "ABC Realty Inc." in the header. Left-align the text "Prepared by *your name*" in the footer, along with a right-aligned page number. Substitute your name for the italicized text in the footer.

k. View the document using Print Preview.

l. Print the document.

m. Save the document as "Budget 1997" to the Data Files location. Keep the document open for use in the next exercise.

4. In this exercise you practice using some commands from previous sessions as well as document formatting commands.

a. Ensure that "Budget 1997" appears in the document area.

b. Change to a Normal view.

c. Set the following page dimensions:

Paper Size:	Letter
Paper Orientation:	Portrait
Top Margin:	1 inch
Bottom Margin:	1 inch
Left Margin:	1 inch
Right Margin:	1 inch

```
                          ABC REALTY INC.

                                                     1997

       Revenue
            Commercial Properties          $125,500,000
            Residential Properties           35,000,000
            Leased Properties                   875,000

       Total Revenue                        $161,375,000

       Expenses
            Insurance                           $50,000
            Salaries                            750,000
            Commissions                      15,500,000
            Office Supplies                      25,000
            Office Equipment                     20,000
            Utilities                            15,000
            Leased Automobiles                   50,000
            Travel                              250,000
            Advertising & Promotion          25,000,000

       Total Expenses                        41,660,000

       Net Income                          $119,715,000
```

d.   Enter the information in Figure 4.24. (*Hint*: Use tabs.)

e.   Preview the document.

f.   Print the document.

g.   Save the document to the Data Files location, replacing the original version.

h.   Close the document.

5.   On your own, create an outline describing a course you would like to take, either one that is currently offered at your school or an entirely new course. The description should consist of a cover page and two additional pages. Ensure that the correct page number and other pertinent information prints on pages two and three. Describe the topics/tasks/activities that should take place each week in a 15-week semester. Save the outline as "On Your Own-7" to your Data Files location and then print it. *Extra Credit*: Create the outline in Outline view and then output it to a PowerPoint presentation. Print the PowerPoint presentation.

GINO'S PIZZA KITCHEN

(*Note*: In the following case problems, assume the role of the primary characters and perform the same steps that they identify. You may want to re-read the session opening.)

1. After a relaxing Christmas holiday, Larry arrives at the office to find the following note on his desk:

    Larry, I trust you had a wonderful time on Nantucket Island. Sorry to be a pain, but I'd like to see the monthly restaurant report ASAP. This time, please include the current page number and date at the bottom of each page. Also, could you leave some room on the left side of each page so that I have a place to make notes? Thanks. Gino.

    With his favorite mug in tow, Larry heads directly for the coffee machine, planning his strategy along the way. When he returns to his desk, Larry turns on the computer, launches Word, and locates the four manager's reports stored in the Advantage Files location. These files are named "GinoNo," "GinoSo," "GinoEast," and "GinoWest." He loads the four documents into separate windows. He then moves the cursor to the end of the "GinoNo" document. After switching to the "GinoSo" document, Larry copies all the text in this document to the Clipboard. Next, he switches back to the "GinoNo" document, pastes the text into the document, and then performs this same procedure for the "GinoEast" and "GinoWest" documents. When finished, the "GinoNo" window contains the four summary reports. He saves this document as "Gino's-December" to the Data Files location.

    Now that he has a single document to work with, Larry begins by inserting a formatted title on the first page of the report that reads:

    Gino's Pizza Kitchen
    Monthly Summary: December

    Using character formatting commands, Larry makes the text in the long document easier to read. He selects a 1.5-inch gutter so that Gino has a place to make notes and then creates a footer displaying the current date and page number. To ensure that the document's text flows nicely, Larry uses a command to make sure that widows and orphans are suppressed. He then saves the document back to the Data Files location, prints the document, and places a copy on Gino's desk.

2. Larry wants additional practice working with headers, footers, and other document formatting commands. He decides to make a copy of the "Gino's-December" document, stored in the Data Files location. He names the copy "Larry," which he will easily recognize as a practice file.

3. Before giving Gino the yearly summary report, Larry decides to format the document to improve its readability. It currently uses only a single font and doesn't incorporate headers, footers, or page numbers. The report is stored in the Advantage Files location as "Gino1996." Larry also decides to include a title page for the report. When finished, he saves the document as "Gino1996-Revised" to the Data Files location and then prints it for Gino's review.

Microsoft Word 97 for Windows

Increasing Your Productivity

SESSION

5

IRWIN
COMPUTER & INFORMATION TECHNOLOGY

SESSION OUTLINE

Using Wizards to Create Documents
Table Fundamentals
Merging Fundamentals
Customizing Word
Summary
Key Terms
Exercises

INTRODUCTION

Computers are getting really smart! With the right tools, they balance our checkbooks, budget how much we're allowed to spend dining out per month, answer our phones when we're not home, and send faxes in the middle of the night to get the best long-distance rates. But what can a software company do to make a word processor smarter? Microsoft's answer: add Wizards to lead you step-by-step through creating professional-looking letters, resumes, and other documents. In this session, you'll meet some of Word's most popular Wizards.

You will also learn how to create tables for organizing columns and rows of information and how to merge address information from a list of respondents into a standard form letter. The session concludes with a discussion on how to customize Word to best fit your working environment.

CASE STUDY	THE UNION TENNIS CLUB

Jerry Garcia is the manager of the beautiful Union Tennis Club in Fort Lauderdale, Florida. He has worked at the club for three years and runs a very tight operation. The club's Board of Directors is pleased with his performance and he has a good relationship with most of his employees. Also, the ones who pay the bills, the members, find him approachable, capable, responsive, and friendly.

Jerry uses a computer to keep track of the club's finances and membership list. Although primarily self-taught on the computer, Jerry has received some help from a few computer-literate members. Jerry is now preparing to put the name of each member with an overdue account into a Microsoft Word document. He remembers his frustrations when performing this task the last time. First, he had trouble aligning the data for each member. And second, he didn't know how to use Word to send a reminder letter to each person in the list. Instead, he grudgingly used the standard "Overdue Account" form on which he wrote the name of the offending member. Jerry knows there's a better way—he just doesn't know where to begin.

In this session, you and Jerry will learn how to create tables for lining up information, how to merge data with a standard form letter, and customize Word to meet your particular needs.

USING WIZARDS TO CREATE DOCUMENTS

Wizards help you to do your work quicker and more efficiently. Whether you need to write a term paper or create an agenda for tomorrow's meeting, a **wizard** gets you started and headed in the right direction. It's not necessary to understand how a wizard works; but it is important to know that wizards are available and easily accessible. You can select from a variety of wizards to create specialized documents, as summarized in Table 5.1.

	Name	*Description*
TABLE 5.1 Some of Word's Wizards	Envelope	Creates a single envelope or multiple envelopes for a mailing list
	Fax	Creates a fax cover sheet; formatting options include Professional, Contemporary, and Elegant
	Letter	Creates the structure for a normal, contemporary, or professional letter format or a newsletter.
	Mailing Label	Creates a single page of labels or multiple pages
	Memo	Creates a standard memo with an optional distribution list
	Resume	Creates an entry-level, chronological, functional, or professional resume

Because the documents created by wizards are based on standard document templates, you can easily edit and format them once they've been created. A **template** is a predesigned and preformatted document into which you put your own information. Word comes with many document templates that you can fill in directly including: Contemporary Resume, Elegant Resume, Contemporary Letter, Professional Letter, Elegant Memo, and Contemporary Report, to name a few. With a little more education and experience, you can also learn how to customize your own templates.

IN ADDITION DOWNLOADING ADDITIONAL TEMPLATES AND WIZARDS FROM THE WEB

 If you have access to the World Wide Web, you can download additional templates and wizards from Microsoft's Web site. To do this:

1. CHOOSE: Help, Microsoft on the Web

2. CHOOSE: Free Stuff

Then follow the instructions on the Web page to download the files you want.

To access a wizard or template, you choose the File, New command, select the appropriate tab from the New dialog box, and then double-click the wizard or template that you want to use. When you invoke a wizard, the selected wizard will display a series of questions and options on the screen regarding how you want the document formatted. On the last page, you click the Finish button and watch as the wizard creates the document right before your eyes.

Although we cannot show you every wizard's creation, we will lead you through one example. In this section, you use a wizard to create a fax cover sheet.

 **Perform the following steps . . .**

1. Open "Software" from the Advantage Files location.

2. To create a new document using a wizard:
   CHOOSE: File, New
   CLICK: *Letters & Faxes* tab
   Your screen should now appear similar to Figure 5.1.

FIGURE 5.1

NEW DIALOG BOX:
LETTERS & FAXES TAB

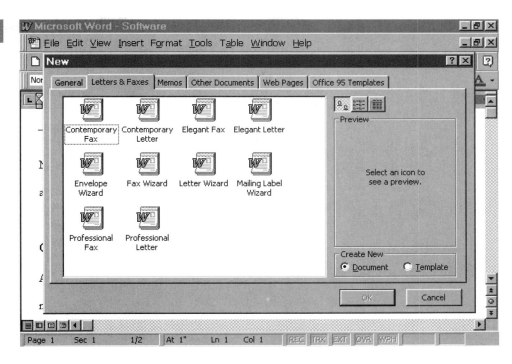

3. Let's start with a relatively simple wizard that is used quite frequently by business people:

DOUBLE-CLICK: Fax Wizard in the *Template* area

The Fax Wizard is launched and presents the initial Fax Wizard screen. Your screen should now appear similar to Figure 5.2. On the left side of the dialog box, you see the steps the Fax Wizard will go through in order to format the final document. To skip to a particular step, you click its name or associated box. Otherwise, if you click Next, the next step will occur.

FIGURE 5.2

FAX WIZARD:INITIAL
SCREEN

4. To proceed to the next screen (Document to Fax):
CLICK: Next button

5. On this screen, ensure that "Software.doc" appears in the *The following document* text box and the *With a cover sheet* option is selected. (*Note:* As you proceed, if you change your mind, you can always review your selections by clicking the Back button or a step in the chart.)

6. Now we're going to skip to the Recipients screen. Since you aren't going to actually fax the document in this exercise, it doesn't matter what you select on the Fax Software screen.
CLICK: Recipients on the left side of the dialog box

7. In the first row, type the name of a friend in the *Name* text box and the corresponding fax number in the *Fax Number* text box. If you prefer fictitious information, refer to Figure 5.3.

FIGURE 5.3

FAX WIZARD: ENTERING
THE RECIPIENT'S
INFORMATION

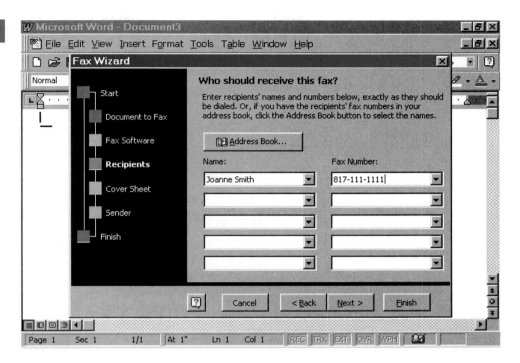

8. To go to the next step (Cover Sheet):
   CLICK: Next button

9. Now the Fax Wizard wants to know whether you prefer a Professional, Contemporary, or Elegant fax cover:
   SELECT: *Elegant* option button (it's not really that elegant!)

10. To go to the next step (Sender):
    CLICK: Next button

11. Now type your information into the Sender screen. If you prefer a fictitious entry, refer to Figure 5.4. You begin by typing in the first text box.

FIGURE 5.4

FAX WIZARD: ENTERING
THE SENDER'S
INFORMATION

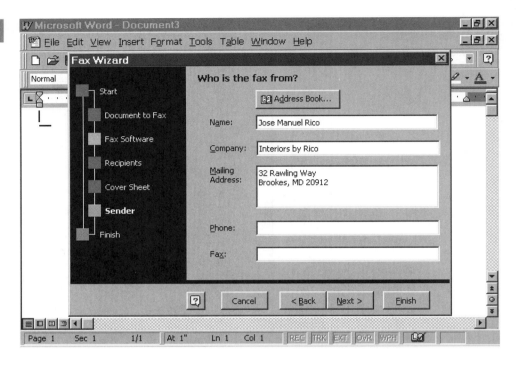

12. To go to the next step (Finish):
    CLICK: Next button

13. To create the cover sheet:
    CLICK: Finish

14. After several seconds (perhaps a minute on slower machines), the fax cover
    document appears in Page Layout view. You are looking at the bottom of
    the document and the Office Assistant appears offering guidance.

15. To remove the Office Assistant from the screen, click the Close icon (🗙)
    in the Office Assistant box.

16. To see the top of the fax cover sheet, drag the scroll box to the top of the
    vertical scroll bar. Your screen should now appear similar to Figure 5.5.
    (*Note:* An anchor may appear on your screen. Anchors are used when fram-
    ing text and graphics, a topic beyond the scope of this guide.)

FIGURE 5.5

PARTIAL VIEW OF THE
COMPLETED FAX COVER
SHEET

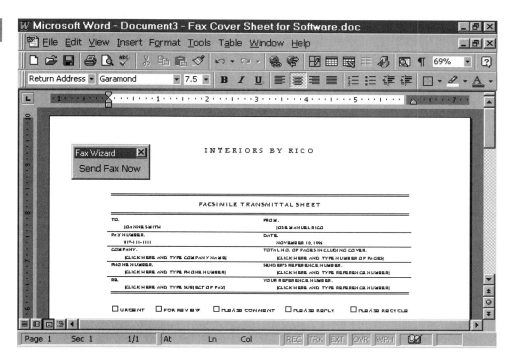

17. Your next step is to complete the fax cover and add any additional comments. Click on any bracketed instructions and either type in the requested information or press the **DELETE** key to remove the comment from the cover sheet.

18. Save the document as "My Fax" to the Data Files location.

19. To print the fax cover:
CLICK: Print button (🖨)

20. Close all documents.

QUICK REFERENCE
Using Wizards

1. **CHOOSE: File, New**

2. **SELECT: a tab in the New dialog box**

3. **SELECT: a wizard from the *Template* area**

4. **Make selections in the Wizard's dialog box and then:**
   CLICK: Next button to proceed

5. **When you are satisfied with the options that you've chosen:**
   CLICK: Finish button

TABLE FUNDAMENTALS

Word provides two methods, tabs and tables, for organizing information using a grid format. This session focuses on Word's table feature. You use a table to line up information into columns and rows. For example, a table works well for creating forms, phone lists, inventory lists, and even financial statements. Although Word provides a Table Wizard, you'll find that creating tables using the toolbar buttons and Word's AutoFormat feature is just as easy and more flexible.

CREATING A TABLE

Put your artist's cap on because Word 97 lets you draw tables. To draw a table, you click the Tables and Borders button (▦) on the Standard toolbar, activating the Tables and Borders toolbar and the Draw Table tool. You simply drag the Draw Table tool on the screen to create the horizontal and vertical lines that make up a table. Using this method, you create each **cell,** the intersection of a row and column, one by one.

If you anticipate that your table will contain many cells, you may consider building the bulk of the table using the Table, Insert command or by clicking the Insert Table button (▦) on the Standard toolbar. With either of these methods you can create a table containing many cells in a few seconds. You place the insertion point where you want the table to appear and then choose the Table, Insert Table command or click the Insert Table button (▦) on the Standard toolbar. You must then specify the desired number of columns and rows.

As a final step, you can use the Tables and Borders toolbar or Word's AutoFormat feature to customize the table to your unique requirements. By the way, don't be concerned if you initially misjudge your requirements, adding and deleting columns and rows is quite straightforward. In this section, you create the cost estimate pictured in Figure 5.6 using the Insert Table button (▦) and the Tables and Borders button (▦).

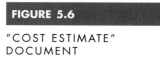

FIGURE 5.6

"COST ESTIMATE" DOCUMENT

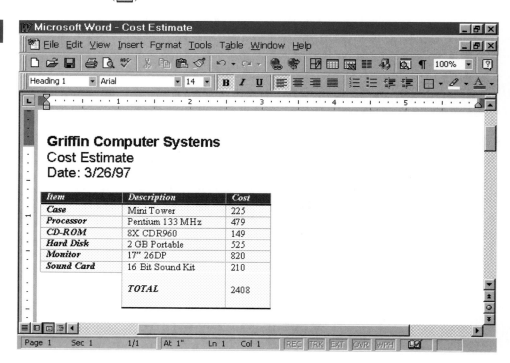

Perform the following steps . . .

1. Open a new document using the New button (🗋). Ensure that you are viewing the document in Normal view.

2. TYPE: `Griffin Computer Systems`
   PRESS: **ENTER**
   TYPE: `Cost Estimate`
   PRESS: **ENTER**
   TYPE: `Date: 3/26/97`
   PRESS: **ENTER** twice

3. To create a table that has 5 rows and 3 columns:
   CLICK: Insert Table button (▦) and hold it down
   DRAG: the mouse pointer downwards until a grid appears
   SELECT: 5 × 3 Table from the pop-up grid menu
   Your screen should now appear similar to Figure 5.7.

FIGURE 5.7

CREATING A TABLE
USING THE MOUSE

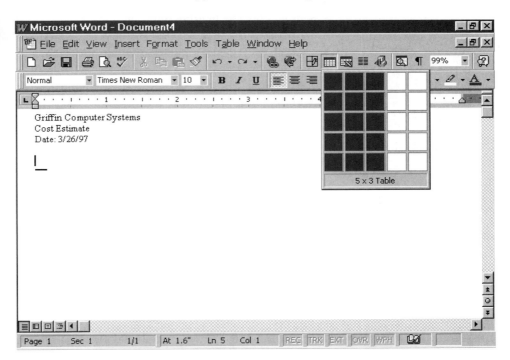

4. Release the mouse button. Word places a table with 5 rows and 3 columns at the insertion point.

QUICK REFERENCE
Creating a Table
Using the Mouse

1. Position the insertion point where you want to insert the table.
2. CLICK: Insert Table button (▦) and hold it down
3. DRAG: the grid pattern to the desired number of rows and columns
4. Release the mouse button.

IN ADDITION CREATING AN EXCEL WORKSHEET IN A WORD DOCUMENT

If you know how to use Excel, you can easily create an Excel worksheet in a Word document using the Insert Microsoft Excel Worksheet ( ) button on the Standard toolbar. You perform the following steps:

1. In the Word document, position the cursor where you want to position the Excel worksheet.

2. CLICK: Insert Microsoft Excel Worksheet ( )

3. By dragging with the mouse, select the size of the table from the pop-up grid menu.

4. Excel's Standard and Formatting toolbars will replace Word's toolbars. Type your data into the worksheet and use Excel's commands to complete the worksheet.

5. CLICK: in the document to return to Word

6. To edit the Excel worksheet, you point to the worksheet and double-click.

ENTERING DATA INTO A TABLE

A table consists of rows and columns. You type information into a cell, which is the intersection of a row and column. To position the insertion point in a cell, you can use the I-beam mouse pointer, press the arrow keys (⬆, ⬇, ⬅, and ➡), or press TAB . If the insertion point is positioned in the rightmost cell of the last row, pressing TAB will automatically add another row to the bottom of the table. You format text within a cell like any other text in the document.

Perform the following steps to enter data.

Perform the following steps . . .

1. With the insertion point in the first cell, let's enter some information into the table, starting with the headings:
   TYPE: `Item`
   PRESS: TAB
   TYPE: `Description`
   PRESS: TAB
   TYPE: `Cost`
   PRESS: TAB
   Notice that the last TAB takes you to the next row in the table.

2. In the same manner as above, enter the following four items under the appropriate headings. You can press TAB to advance to the next cell, or you can try using the arrow keys and mouse pointer:

Item	*Description*	*Cost*
Case	Mini Tower	225
Processor	Pentium 133 MHz	479
Hard Disk	2 GB Portable	525
Monitor	17" 26DP	820

3. With the insertion point in the last cell (820), press the ⬭TAB⬭ key to add another row to the table. (*Note:* If you already pressed ⬭TAB⬭ in the previous step and a new row appeared, move to step 4.)

4. Enter one more item into the table:
TYPE: Sound Card
PRESS: ⬭TAB⬭
TYPE: 16 Bit Sound Kit
PRESS: ⬭TAB⬭
TYPE: 210
PRESS: ⬇
Notice that the insertion point leaves the table with this last keystroke.

5. To add a blank line:
PRESS: ⬭ENTER⬭

6. When you click inside a table, the Insert Table button (▦) changes to the Insert Rows button (⬛). To illustrate:
CLICK: in the fourth row of the table (Hard Disk)
Notice that the Insert Table button (▦) changed to the Insert Rows button (⬛).

7. To insert a row:
CLICK: Insert Rows button (⬛)
A row was inserted above the fourth row.

8. Click in the first cell of the newly inserted row.

9. Type the following information:
TYPE: CD-ROM
PRESS: ⬭TAB⬭
TYPE: 8X CDR960
PRESS: ⬭TAB⬭
TYPE: 149
Your screen should now appear similar to Figure 5.8.

FIGURE 5.8

THE DATA HAS BEEN
ENTERED

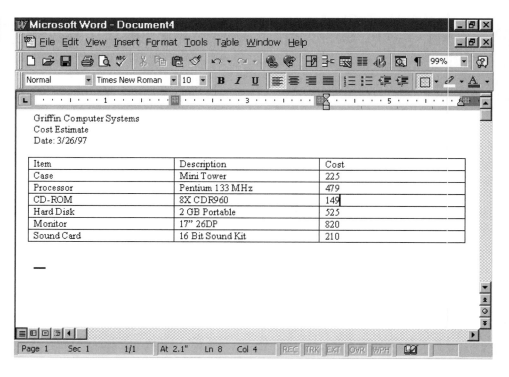

10. In the next few steps, you narrow the columns to better fit the data. Point with the mouse to the vertical border separating the first and second columns. The mouse pointer should change to a double-headed arrow.

11. By referring to Figure 5.6, hold down the mouse button and drag the border to the left. Repeat the procedure for the vertical border between the second and third columns and for the far-right vertical border.

DRAWING A TABLE

In this section, you complete the cost estimate by drawing the total cells at the bottom of the table. Before you can use the Draw Table tool, your document must appear in Page Layout view. If you don't switch to Page Layout view prior to activating the drawing pencil, Word will display a message indicating that you should switch. In this section, you practice drawing a few cells in a table.

Perform the following steps . . .

1. To switch to Page Layout view:
CLICK: Page Layout button (▣)

2. CLICK: Tables and Borders button
Your screen should appear similar to Figure 5.9. The Draw Table tool is activated and the Tables and Borders toolbar appears. Also, the Office Assistant may appear with a helpful tip. (*Note:* The Office Assistant doesn't appear in Figure 5.9.)

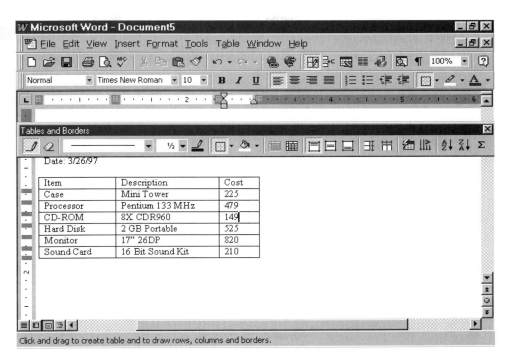

Date: 3/26/97

Item	Description	Cost
Case	Mini Tower	225
Processor	Pentium 133 MHz	479
CD-ROM	8X CDR960	149
Hard Disk	2 GB Portable	525
Monitor	17" 26DP	820
Sound Card	16 Bit Sound Kit	210

Click and drag to create table and to draw rows, columns and borders.

3. If necessary, drag the Tables and Borders toolbar to another area of the screen or reshape it so that you can see more of your document. Also, if the Office Assistant appears:
CLICK: Close icon (☒) in the Office Assistant box

4. To create the outside border of the two cells at the bottom of the table (see Figure 5.6), point to the bottom-left corner of the last cell in the Description column.

5. Hold the mouse button down and, by referring to Figure 5.6, drag downwards and to the right to create the two cells. Your screen should appear similar to Figure 5.10.

FIGURE 5.10

DRAWING A CELL

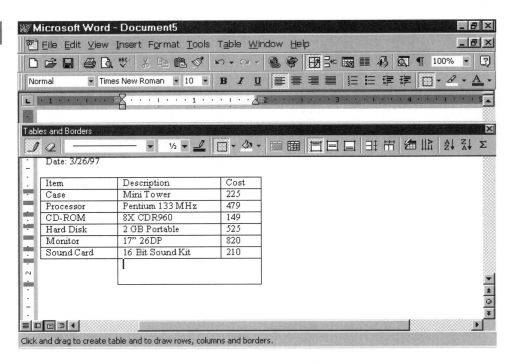

6. The Draw Table tool is still activated. On your own, create the vertical line that will divide the newly inserted cell into two cells.

7. To deactivate the Draw Table tool:
CLICK: Draw Table button (🖉) in the Tables and Borders toolbar
The Tables and Borders toolbar no longer appears.

8. CLICK: in the leftmost cell
TYPE: TOTAL
PRESS: (TAB)

9. To total the amounts above, use the AutoSum button (Σ) on the Tables and Borders toolbar.
RIGHT-CLICK: a toolbar button
CHOOSE: Tables and Borders
CLICK: AutoSum button (Σ)
A total of the amounts above automatically appears in the cell.

10. In this step, you center vertically the data in the newly inserted cells.
SELECT: the two cells at the bottom of the table
CLICK: Center Vertically button (🗉) on the Tables and Borders toolbar

11. Close the Tables and Borders toolbar.

12. Save the document as "Cost Estimate" to the Data Files location.

FORMATTING A TABLE

With Word's Table AutoFormat command, you can format your tables in just a few keystrokes or mouse clicks. Using the menu, you first place the insertion point in any cell of the table and then choose the Table, Table AutoFormat command. An easier method is to right-click the desired table and choose the Table AutoFormat command from its shortcut menu. Either way, the dialog box in Figure 5.11 appears, from which you can select one of over 30 professionally designed formats.

FIGURE 5.11

TABLE AUTOFORMAT
DIALOG BOX

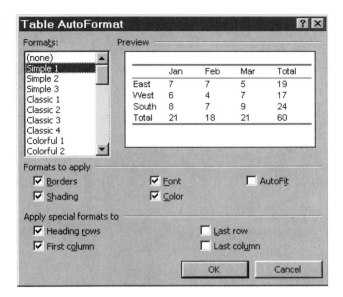

Let's demonstrate how to format a table.

Perform the following steps . . .

1. Ensure that the insertion point appears in the table. If not, move the insertion point into the table using the mouse or arrow keys.

2. To format the table:
   CHOOSE: Table, Table AutoFormat
   The dialog box in Figure 5.11 appears. (*Note:* Remember that you can also right-click the table to display the shortcut menu and then choose Table Autoformat from the menu.)

3. To view the formatting options:
   PRESS: ⬇ repeatedly, pausing between each press to view the formatting characteristics shown in the *Preview* area

4. SELECT: Colorful 2 in the *Formats* list box
   PRESS: (**ENTER**) or CLICK: OK
   The table is immediately formatted using the Colorful 2 options.

5. Let's format the titles at the top of the page before proceeding:
   SELECT: Griffin Computer Systems
   SELECT: Arial (or another font) from the *Font* drop-down list ([Times New Roman ▾])
   SELECT: 14 point from the *Font Size* drop-down list ([10 ▾])
   CLICK: Bold button ([**B**])

6. Format the "Cost Estimate" and "Date: 3/26/97" information using the same commands as in step 5, but don't apply the bold attribute.

7. CLICK: near the end of the document to remove the highlighting
Your screen should now appear similar to Figure 5.6. (*Note:* The screen in Figure 5.6 is zoomed to 100%.)

8. Save the "Cost Estimate" document to the Data Files location, replacing the original version.

9. Close all the open documents in the document area.

10. Remove the Tables and Borders toolbar.

QUICK REFERENCE
Using Table AutoFormat

1. **Position the insertion point in the table you want to format.**
2. **CHOOSE: Table, Table AutoFormat**
3. **SELECT: formatting options from the *Formats* list box**
4. **PRESS:** ENTER **or CLICK: OK**

IN ADDITION CREATING COLUMNS

Tables are best used for keeping text, numbers, or dates aligned in a grid format. Word also provides you with the capability to create *newspaper columns,* also called *snaking columns,* whereby text wraps automatically to the top of the next column when it reaches the bottom of the current column.

To create columns, choose Format, Columns from the Menu bar or click the Columns button (▦) on the Standard toolbar. For more information, choose Help, Contents and Index from the Menu bar. Click the *Index* tab and then type **columns.** A list of topics will appear.

IN ADDITION INSERTING AN ACCESS TABLE IN WORD

Perform the following steps in Word:

1. In your Word document, position the cursor where you want the Access table to appear.

2. Display the Database toolbar.

3. CLICK: Insert Database (▣) on the Database toolbar

4. CLICK: Get Data command button

5. CLICK: MS Access Databases in the *Files of type* box

6. Select a database in the *filename* box and then click the Open command button.

7. Click the *Tables or Queries* tab and then select a table or query.

8. If you want Word to format the table for you:
CLICK: Table AutoFormat command button

9. Choose how you want the table formatted and then click OK.

10. To copy the Access data into Word:
CLICK: Insert Data command button

11. Select the records to include in the Insert Data dialog box.

12. If you want the inserted Access data to be linked to Access so that the data is updated automatically as it changes in Access:
SELECT: Insert data as field check box

MERGING FUNDAMENTALS

Have you ever received a letter from a company or organization that you knew absolutely nothing about? Was your name typed in the salutation and perhaps mentioned in the body of the letter? This kind of document is called a *form letter.* Your name, along with thousands of others, is stored in a mailing list and placed into specific locations in a letter through a process called **merging**. Merging requires two files: the **data source** and the **main document**. The data source contains variable data, such as names and addresses, to be merged with the main document or form letter.

PREPARING A MERGE OPERATION

Word provides a utility called the Mail Merge Helper that leads you through performing a mail merge from scratch. In addition to creating form letters, the Mail Merge Helper can assist you with printing mailing labels, envelopes, and catalogs. You start the Mail Merge Helper by choosing the Tools, Mail Merge command from the menu. In this section, you will perform a simple merge of an employee mailing list with an interoffice memo.

Next, you merge a list of names with a memo.

Perform the following steps . . .

1. Open a new document using the New button (▢). Ensure that you are viewing the document in Normal view.

2. To launch the Mail Merge Helper:
   CHOOSE: Tools, Mail Merge
   Your screen should now appear similar to Figure 5.12.

FIGURE 5.12

MAIL MERGE HELPER

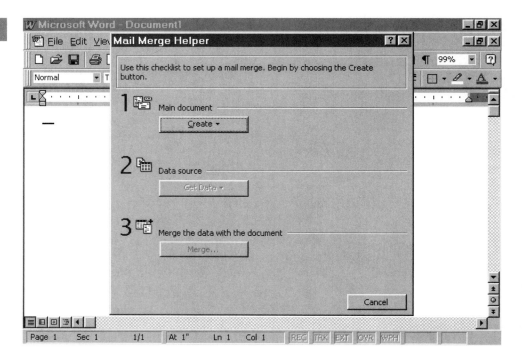

3. The Mail Merge Helper provides three steps as a checklist for performing a mail merge. The first step, according to the dialog box, is to create a main document file. To proceed:
SELECT: Create command button
A pop-up menu appears with four possible options: Form Letters, Mailing Labels, Envelopes, and Catalog.

4. To perform a merge for a letter or other such document (i.e., memo):
CHOOSE: Form Letters from the pop-up menu

5. To use the active document for creating the main document file:
SELECT: Active Window command button
Notice that the information you selected appears below the *Main document* area in the Mail Merge Helper dialog box.

6. Because you are starting this mail merge operation from scratch, you must create a new data source file. To proceed:
SELECT: Get Data command button
CHOOSE: Create Data Source from the pop-up menu
Your screen should now appear similar to Figure 5.13.

FIGURE 5.13

CREATE DATA SOURCE
DIALOG BOX

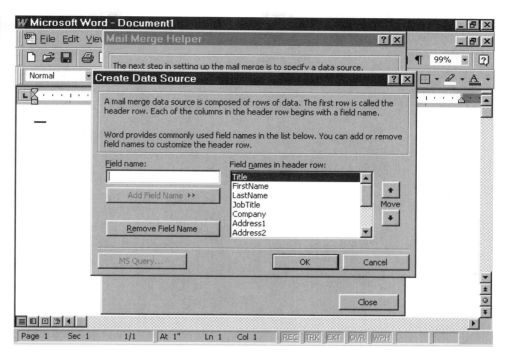

7. You use the Create Data Source dialog box to define the information you will be merging with the main document file. For the employee mailing list, you require entry blanks (also called **fields**) for their first name, last name, city, state, postal or zip code, and phone number. Fortunately, these fields are among the defaults provided in the *Field names in header row* list box. To remove the other field names in the list box, you highlight a field name and then select the Remove Field Name command button. Do the following:
   SELECT: Title in the *Field names in header row* list box
   SELECT: Remove Field Name command button

8. Using the procedure outlined in the previous step, remove all the field names in the *Field names in header row* list box, except for FirstName, LastName, City, State, PostalCode, and WorkPhone.

9. To proceed to the next step:
   PRESS: (ENTER) or CLICK: OK
   The Save As dialog box should appear.

10. Save the data source file as "Mail List" to the Data Files location.
   After Word finishes saving the file, it displays a dialog box giving you the choice of adding information to the data source or working in the main document.

11. To add the employee information to the "Mail List" data source file:
   SELECT: Edit Data Source command button
   Your screen should now appear similar to Figure 5.14.

FIGURE 5.14

DATA FORM DIALOG BOX

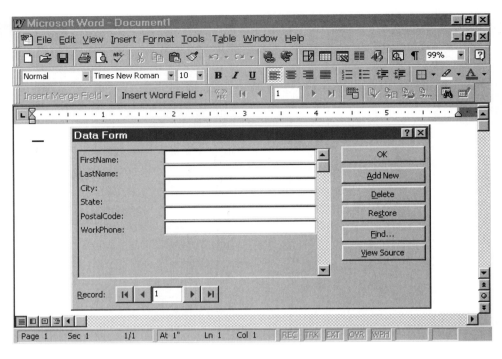

12. Enter the following information using the Data Form dialog box. To advance to the next field, you press ⌷TAB⌷ or use the mouse. When you reach the WorkPhone field, you press ⌷ENTER⌷ or click the Add New command button to add a new employee to the data file.

FirstName	LastName	City	State	PostalCode	WorkPhone
Janos	Sagi	Boston	MA	02116	617-552-4224
Becky	McFee	Chicago	IL	60637	312-654-9871
Sima	Veiner	Toronto	ON	M5B 2H1	416-599-1080
Jack	Yee	Seattle	WA	98004	206-787-3554

13. To finish adding information to the data source file:
SELECT: OK command button
You are placed in the main document file, where you will begin editing the form letter. Notice the Merge toolbar that appears below the Formatting toolbar.

14. Let's create a memo to the four employees in the data source file:
TYPE: DATE:
PRESS: ⌷TAB⌷ twice
TYPE: *current date*
PRESS: ⌷ENTER⌷ twice
TYPE: TO:
PRESS: ⌷TAB⌷ twice

15. To have Word automatically substitute the names of the employees into this memo, you need to specify the merge fields that contain the information:
CLICK: Insert Merge Field button in the Merge toolbar
CHOOSE: FirstName from the drop-down menu
PRESS: Space Bar
CLICK: Insert Merge Field button
CHOOSE: LastName from the drop-down menu

16. Now let's add the merge field codes for address information:
PRESS: (ENTER) to advance one line
PRESS: (TAB) twice
CLICK: Insert Merge Field button
CHOOSE: City from the drop-down menu
TYPE: , (a comma)
PRESS: Space Bar
CLICK: Insert Merge Field button
CHOOSE: State from the drop-down menu
PRESS: (ENTER) twice

17. TYPE: FROM:
PRESS: (TAB) twice
TYPE: *your name*
PRESS: (ENTER) four times

18. Enter the body text of the memo:
TYPE: Please be advised that the meeting has been postponed until the 4th of January.

19. Save the document as "Mail Merge Memo" to the Data Files location. Your screen should now appear similar to Figure 5.15.

FIGURE 5.15

"MAIL MERGE MEMO"
DOCUMENT

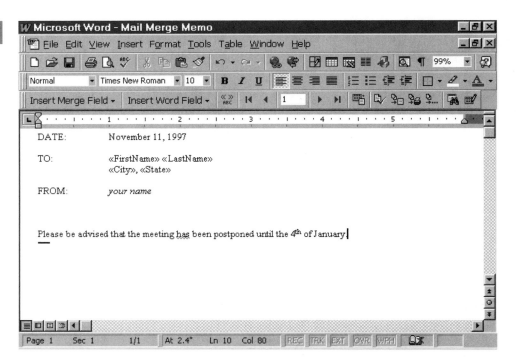

20. To return to the Mail Merge Helper dialog box:
    CHOOSE: Tools, Mail Merge
    (*Note:* You can also click the Mail Merge Helper button (▦) on the Merge toolbar.) The filenames of the main document and the data source file should appear below their respective steps in the dialog box.

21. Proceed to the next section.

QUICK REFERENCE

Preparing a Mail
Merge Operation

1. **CHOOSE: Tools, Mail Merge**

2. **Specify a main document file.**

3. **Specify an existing data source file or create a new data source file.**

4. **If necessary, add information to the data source file.**

5. **Edit the main document, inserting merge fields as desired.**

IN ADDITION USING AN EXCEL OR ACCESS DATA SOURCE WHEN PERFORMING A MERGE
OPERATION

1. CHOOSE: Tools, Mail Merge

2. Specify a main document file.

3. Specify an Excel worksheet file or an Access database file as the data source.

4. Specify the desired worksheet range, or Access table or query, containing the data for merging.

5. Edit the main document, inserting merge fields as desired.

6. On the merge toolbar, select either the Merge to New Document button or the Merge to Printer button.

PERFORMING THE MERGE

Once the data source file and the main document file have been created, you are ready to perform the merge. The output of the merge is typically sent to a new document or to the printer. If there are only a few records in the data source file, you may prefer to merge to a new document, save the document for review, and then print the document at a later time. If there are 2,500 records in the data source file and the main document file consists of ten pages, then merging the two files would result in a 25,000-page document—an unacceptable length by most standards. In this case, merging directly to the printer is your best option.

Let's now demonstrate how to perform a merge.

Perform the following steps . . .

1. With the Mail Merge Helper dialog box displayed:
SELECT: Merge command button
Your screen should now appear similar to Figure 5.16.

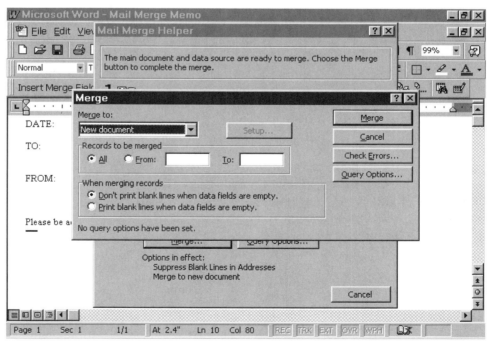

2. In the *Merge to* drop-down list box:
SELECT: New Document

3. To perform the merge:
CLICK: Merge command button
The data source file is merged with the main document file and the result appears in a separate document.

4. Save the new document as "Merged Documents" to the Data Files location.

5. Close all the open documents in the document area. When asked to save changes to your documents, respond yes to all dialog boxes.

QUICK REFERENCE
Performing the Merge

1. **In the Mail Merge Helper dialog box:**
   SELECT: Merge command button
2. **In the Merge dialog box:**
   SELECT: Merge command button

CUSTOMIZING WORD

This section introduces you to some of the basic customization options available in Word 97. This section is not intended to be an all-inclusive discussion.

CHANGING WORD'S DEFAULT SETTINGS

You modify Word's default settings in the Options dialog box, accessed by choosing the Tools, Options command. There are a variety of customization topics contained in this dialog box. For example, you can remove the Status bar and scroll bars from the application window, display the Paragraph symbol on-screen at all times, change Word's default mode to Overtype, and tell the Spell Checker to ignore words in uppercase. This section is a guided tour of only some of these topics, providing you with enough information to explore them on your own.

Let's now demonstrate how to change default settings.

Perform the following steps . . .

1. Open a new document.

2. To access the Options dialog box:
   CHOOSE: Tools, Options
   Notice the topical tabs that appear in this dialog box.

3. Let's review the View settings first:
   CLICK: *View* tab
   There are three primary groups on this page: *Show*, *Nonprinting Characters*, and *Window*. The *Show* group provides an option for viewing your document using a draft font. One of our favorite features is the ability to display just the Paragraph symbol on-screen without having to show all the other hidden characters and codes. You select this option from the *Nonprinting Characters* group. The *Window* group lets you remove the Status bar and scroll bars from the application window to increase your document viewing area.

4. CLICK: *Save* tab
The most popular save options (shown in Figure 5.17) include:
- *Always create backup copy* check box
- *Allow fast saves* check box
- *Save AutoRecover info every* check box

Although relatively self-explanatory, you can find more information about each option by clicking the question mark icon (🔲) in the Title bar and then clicking an element.

FIGURE 5.17

OPTIONS DIALOG BOX: SAVE TAB

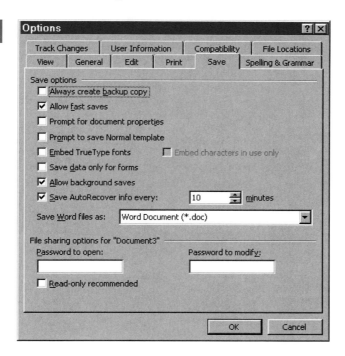

5. CLICK: *File Locations* tab
To specify where on your disk you would like Word to look for documents, highlight the Documents option and then select the Modify command button. Word uses this information in the Open dialog box.

6. CLICK: *Spelling & Grammar* tab
If you work with technical terms, abbreviations, figures, or Internet addresses, you will appreciate the three check boxes on this page for ignoring information during a spelling check. For example, when the *Ignore words in UPPERCASE* and *Ignore words with numbers* check boxes are selected, the Spell Checker progresses through a document without stopping on text like RAM, CPU, or 486. Figure 5.18 provides an example of the Spelling and Grammar options.

FIGURE 5.18

OPTIONS DIALOG BOX:
SPELLING TAB

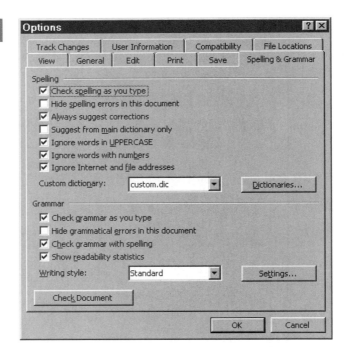

7. To cancel our whirlwind tour through the Options dialog box:
PRESS: (**ESC**) or CLICK: Cancel

IN ADDITION OPTIONS DIALOG BOX: FOR MORE INFORMATION

To find out more information about any setting in the Options dialog box, select the tab of the page you want to learn more about and then

click the question mark icon (**?**). You can click any element in the dialog box to display helpful information.

UNDERSTANDING MACROS

A **macro** is a collection of keystrokes that has been recorded in order to automate a particular sequence of tasks. Once recorded, the procedure or task may be executed again and again by simply selecting the macro from a list or by pressing a shortcut key combination. You can also assign macros to buttons on the toolbar or create new pull-down menu commands. Macros are usually created to cut down on the amount of time and effort required to perform repetitive tasks specific to your work.

IN ADDITION MACROS: FOR MORE INFORMATION

 Creating macros is beyond the scope of this session, but definitely not beyond your grasp to learn and use in your documents. To find out more about macros, choose Help, Con- tents and Index from the Menu bar. Click the *Index* tab and then type `macros`. A list of topics will appear.

Summary

This session introduced you to creating complex documents using wizards. Word 97 provides wizards for creating many types of common documents including fax covers, resumes, letters, envelopes, and memos. Using the Fax Wizard in this session, you produced an attractive fax cover sheet within minutes. You also created and formatted tables in this session for organizing information into rows and columns.

With Word's Mail Merge Helper, you can easily produce form letters. A form letter is a standard document where only the addressee or other variable information changes. With the variable information entered into a data source file, only a single form letter needs to be created. The process of merging takes the information from the data source file and inserts it into the correct locations in the form letter. In this session, you merged names and addresses into a standard memo.

The session concluded with a brief discussion on customizing Word's default settings. Table 5.2 provides a list of the commands and procedures covered in this session.

TABLE 5.2	*Task Description*	*Menu Command*	*Toolbar Button*
Command Summary	Access wizards for creating new documents	File, New	
	Create or insert a table	Table, Insert Table	▦
	Draw a table	Table, Draw Table	▦
	Format a table based on predefined formatting guidelines	Table, Table AutoFormat	
	Start the Mail Merge Helper to lead you through a mail merge	Tools, Mail Merge	
	Access Word's default settings	Tools, Options	

KEY TERMS

cell

The intersection of a column and row in a table.

data source

A document file that uses a table to capture and store variable information for the merge process.

fields

In a data source file, the entry blanks or individual pieces of information. In a table, rows are complete records for items or people and columns are fields or pieces of information in each record.

macro

A collection of keystrokes that is recorded for playback at a later date. A macro enables you to perform a series of operations by pressing a shortcut key combination or clicking a toolbar button.

main document

A type of form letter document used by Word in the merge process. The main document file contains codes to insert information from the data source file.

merging

The process of taking information from a data source file and inserting it into a form letter or main document file, one record at a time. The results from merging these two files can be sent to a file or the printer.

template

A predesigned form into which you can enter your own information.

wizard

A Word feature that provides step-by-step assistance through the document creation process.

EXERCISES

SHORT ANSWER

1. List nine wizards that are available in Word 97.

2. How would you create a resume using a wizard?

3. When would you use a table in a document?

4. Name three methods for creating a table.

5. What is the quickest method for formatting a table?

6. Explain the merge process.

7. What is a data source file?

8. List two options for where the results of a print merge can be sent.

9. How do you tell Word to display the Paragraph symbol on-screen without displaying the other nonprinting characters and codes?

10. How do you create a macro?

HANDS-ON

(*Note*: Ensure that you know the location of your Advantage Files and where to store your Data Files. If necessary, ask your instructor or lab assistant for additional information.)

1. In the following exercise, you create and format a table.

   a. Open a new document.

   b. Create the document appearing in Figure 5.19.

current date

Mr. Roland Garros
Clay Supplies Inc.
1091 Panorama Ridge
Houston, TX   76798

Dear Mr. Garros:

Per your request, I am providing a list of the items that you ordered for your office last Wednes-day.

Please confirm the order by placing your initials beside each item in the column provided, and then fax this letter back to me at 817-747-1234.

Yours sincerely,
Grand Slam Computer Sales

your name
Account Representative

c. Insert the following table between the first and second paragraph.

Client Initial	Qty	Description	Total Price
	5	Laser Printers	$10,250.00
	5	Printer Cables	76.00
	20	3.5" Diskettes	30.00
	5	Windows 95	450.00

d. Make the headings in the table bold.

e. Add a new row at the bottom of the table and enter the following:

		TOTAL COST	$10,806.00

f. Apply a predefined format of your choice to the table using the Table, Table AutoFormat command.

g. Save the document as "Roland Garros" to the Data Files location.

h. Print the document.

i. Close the document.

2. In this exercise, you create a main document file and a data source file, and then perform a merge of the two documents to create a third file.

a. Open a new document.

b. CHOOSE: Tools, Mail Merge

c. Use the active window as the main document file.

d. Create a new file for the data source.

e. Use the following fields for the data file: FirstName, LastName, Address1, City, State, ZipCode.

f. Save the data source as "Customer Data" to the Data Files location.

g. Enter the following information into the data source file.

FirstName	LastName	Address1	City	State	ZipCode
Elliot	Lepinski	898 Burrard Ave.	Louisville	KY	40205
Red	Robinson	235 Johnson St.	Washington	DC	20052
Elaine	Maynard	1005 West 9th St.	Baton Rouge	LA	70803
Ranjitt	Singh	122 Cordova Ave.	Tacoma	WA	98416
William	Delaney	36 Primore Road	Wichita	KS	67208
Francisco	Ortez	875 Broadway	Albuquerque	NM	87131
Alice	Chan	29 Redmond Road	San Francisco	CA	92182
Jessica	Thomas	909 West 18th St.	Brooklyn	NY	11225
Jimmy	Kazo	888 East 8th Ave.	Billings	MT	59101

h. Create the document appearing in Figure 5.20. Do not type the merge codes. Use the Insert Merge Field button to add each merge code, such as <<FirstName>>, to the document.

current date

<<FirstName>> <<LastName>>
<<Address1>>
<<City>>, <<State>>   <<ZipCode>>

Dear <<FirstName>>:

                        We're Moving!

Please be informed that as of August 31st we are moving to new premises located at 8030 United Boulevard in Boston.

We are looking forward to this move with great anticipation. Because of your continued support, we are expanding our training facilities to accommodate two training rooms and a boardroom.

As a result of this move, we will be closed from the third week in August to the end of September. An invitation to the Open House will be forwarded to you, <<FirstName>>, as soon as we are settled.

Let us know if we can do anything for you!

Sincerely,

your name
President

i. Save the main file as "Customer Form" to the Data Files location.

j. Perform the merge to a new document, using the Mail Merge Helper. Print out the first page of the new document

k. Save the new file as "Customer - Merged Documents" to the Data Files location.

l. Close the document.

3. Guess what? You have been asked to distribute a memo to your entire class describing an upcoming field trip to Microsoft Corporation in Redmond, Washington. Perform the following steps.

   a. Use the Memo Wizard to create the memo.

   b. When requested, include your name and initials in the memo.

   c. Save the memo to your Data Files location as "Class Memo."

   d. Print the "Class Memo" document.

   e. Close the document.

4. On your own, create a form letter that describes what you've been up to lately. As you proceed, keep the following in mind:

   a. Choose Tools, Mail Merge to begin.

   b. Create a data source that contains the names and addresses of five or more family members and/or friends.

   c. Save the data source as "Friends" to the Data Files location.

   d. Create the form letter document. Insert the merge codes you defined in step a using the Insert Merge Field button.

   e. Save the main file as "My News" to the Data Files location.

   f. Perform the merge to a new document, using the Mail Merge Helper.

   g. Print the documents, but don't save them.

   h. Close all the documents.

5. On your own, create a table of names and addresses, recipes, expenses, To Do tasks, or whatever you would find useful. Without obscuring your data, incorporate as many formatting features into the table as you can. Save the table as "On Your Own-9" to your Data Files location.

CASE PROBLEMS   THE UNION TENNIS CLUB

(*Note*: In the following case problems, assume the role of the primary characters and perform the same steps that they identify. You may want to re-read the session opening.)

1. Now that he knows how to create tables, Jerry isn't dreading the task at hand. Nine members of the Union Tennis Club have overdue accounts and he must put their names and addresses (see below) into a table. When finished, he saves the file as "Overdue Accounts" to the Data Files location. (*Note*: Include the table headings in the first row of the table.)

FirstName	LastName	Address1	City	State	PostalCode
Muriel	Britzky	3710 Bush Street	San Francisco	CA	94111
Myron	Drexler	1485 Sonoma Hwy	Sonoma	CA	96555
Julie	Davis	100 Bosley Lane	New York	NY	90000
Mitch	Kaplanoff	20 Cactus Lane	Palm Desert	CA	98888
Michael	Reynolds	17 Windy Way	Lincoln	MA	09111
Jacob	Raggio	P.O. Box 145	Evergreen	CO	89777
Mary	Timberlake	151 Greer Road	Evanston	IL	60201
Todd	Bowman	200 Union Street	San Francisco	CA	14441
Valli	Terris	1871 Orrinton Ave	Chicago	IL	87555

2. Since he has already created the table of overdue members, Jerry decides to create a reminder letter complete with merge codes. During the process, Jerry selects "Open Data Source" to tell Microsoft Word where to "get" the data and specifies his "Overdue Accounts" document in the Data Files location. After creating the form letter, Jerry saves it to the Data Files location as "UTC - Form Letter." He then performs the merge and prints out the form letters. Because he's concerned about disk space on his computer, he doesn't save the merged form letters as a document to the Data Files location.

3. Jerry wants to include a table in the upcoming newsletter that lists the sale items available in the club's tennis shop. These items include:

Item	Description	Cost
Tennis Racket	Wilson Hammer	$139.00
Tennis Shirts	UTC logo	$14.95
Tennis Shorts	Navy-Mens	$21.99
Visors	White	$7.50
Tennis Balls	Wilson	$2.00
Tennis Bag	Penn	$24.99

After creating the table, Jerry formats and then prints it for the newsletter. He saves it to the Data Files location as "UTC - Sale" and closes the document. With his desk clear, Jerry pokes his head out of his office and asks politely: "Tennis, anyone?"

Appendix

Microsoft Word 97 for Windows Toolbar Summary

STANDARD

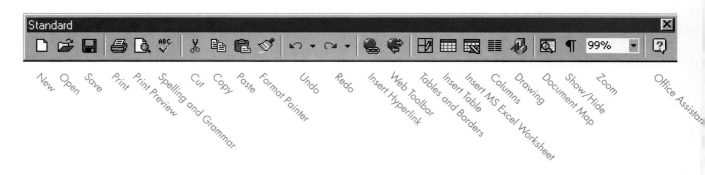

FORMATTING

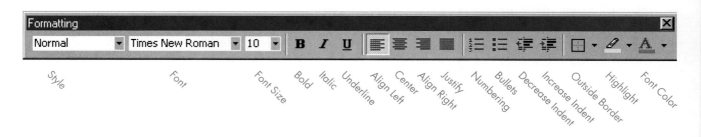

DRAWING

PICTURE

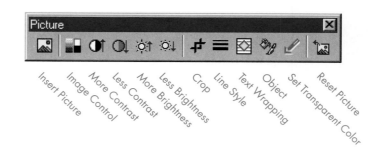

TABLES

WORDART

Index

The page numbers in boldface indicate Quick Reference procedures.